HOW TO GIGGLE

HOW TO GIGGLE

A GUIDE TO TAKING LIFE LESS SERIOUSLY

PAIGE DESORBO   **HANNAH BERNER**

SIMON
ELEMENT

NEW YORK   AMSTERDAM/ANTWERP   LONDON
TORONTO   SYDNEY/MELBOURNE   NEW DELHI

**SIMON
ELEMENT**

An Imprint of Simon & Schuster, LLC
1230 Avenue of the Americas
New York, NY 10020

TO OUR MOMS, DAPHNE, BUTTER, AND THE GIGGLERS

CONTENTS

ARE YOU PAIGE OR HANNAH CODED?

PAIGE

Uber XL

Limited Too

Black cat

Miranda Priestly

Ballet-pink nails

Chandeliers

Mint Juul

Long fingers

Short bob

Yankees

Capri

Scorpio

Churros

Tablescapes

Upper West Side

No Pants

BOTH

Chicken Parm

Loving our moms

Revenge

Beta-Blockers

Pooping our pants

Voice notes

Bed rotting

Not calling back
if FaceTime drops

Loving our cats

Peppermint
mocha

Tube tops

Cottage cheese

Mid-century modern

Peach tea Snapple

Sparkly eye shadow

Tennis

Screenshots

Long torso

Vintage shopping

Fantasy football

Dublin

Lower East Side

Scallion cream cheese
on a bagel

The worm

Leo

HANNAH

GIGGLY

SQUAD

ORIGIN

STORY

01

DON'T WASTE A MINUTE NOT BEING HAPPY. IF ONE WINDOW CLOSES, RUN TO THE NEXT WINDOW—OR BREAK DOWN A DOOR.

—Brooke Shields

TO BE FULLY TRANSPARENT, we were nervous about writing a book because Paige can't spell to save her life and Hannah can't read anything longer than an Instagram caption because she has the attention span of a small squirrel. But we love a challenge. We were also procrastinating about starting the book because writing the first line seemed like so much pressure, but then we realized you probably judged us already by the cover (dad joke) and if you made it to the first page after that, congrats! You are officially reading books in your leisure time, which is so chic of you. It's giving French girl with ballet slippers drinking an espresso with no problems. But if the commitment of reading an entire book is making you anxious, don't worry; it's basically a picture book with a bunch of lists.

So what the hell are you about to read? This book is about how two lost souls have found some happiness and success in this harsh world by taking life less seriously. We want to share with you our friendship, stories, strong opinions, secrets, and, of course, lots of giggles.

It may come as a surprise, but like many things in our world, such as colonization and crypto, the term *Giggly Squad* was created by a man. But after the words were yelled into the universe, the girlies took the name and ran with it (we don't actually run, so picture more of a brisk walk). But before we explain this canon event, we have to start with our origin story.

HANNAH'S VERSION

It was a brisk autumn day in 2018. I don't know what month it was, but I know Paige was wearing boots, so I would guess November. I was working at a media company as a comedy video producer. It was the first job I actually liked. The job I had before was cold-calling sales, and I would dread going to the office and then spend half the day in the bathroom having nervous diarrhea. But this new job was creative, and even though it paid terribly, I finally found a career path I was excited about. I loved to create and make people laugh. I was writing memes and scripts, casting comics, acting, and editing videos. I wanted to work there the rest of my life. I got fired after only a year or so, like most of my jobs, but at the time, I was on top of the world.

One day, the boss told me she followed someone online who did pop culture news updates every morning on Insta stories. She showed me the videos, and the girl was pretty, with a sarcastic sense of humor. We decided to ask her to come in to have a meeting with the team. A couple days later, I noticed a dainty girl with a sleek black bob wearing a black outfit and knee-high boots standing at the door. I had no idea where the boss was, but I quickly stood up to greet her. She looked strong but shy, like a black cat. Fun fact about me, I love black cats. I jumped up from my little desk and walked toward her to say hi. She immediately had a big smile on her face, and I told her I had no clue where the boss was but she could sit and wait with me in our office kitchen. I don't remember what I was saying to her, but I remember that she had an easy, contagious laugh and she seemed to find me entertaining. The giggles had begun. She started writing freelance articles for the company, but I didn't see her very much.

A couple months later, I got an unexpected DM from a casting director. I assumed there was a high chance that this was an attempt to kidnap me into a human trafficking ring, but I hopped on the call with this random guy anyway. He said he had seen my videos and thought I could potentially be a good fit for a show about New Yorkers. He told me that he was also talking to Paige and Jordan (who also worked with me) because he wanted to cast people who knew each other. I didn't think much of it because being on

The makeup artist took this BTS pic of my first ever Bravo confessional. Why is it giving Mona Lisa?

a television show felt like a fever dream and I also never thought I would do reality TV. I was terrified of confrontation and couldn't tell you the last time I had any real drama in a friend group. But I was twenty-six years old and my brain had just fully formed, so I was ready to try anything. A couple weeks later, I was asked to go on a Zoom meeting, where they asked me a lot of questions about how I felt about people on the cast. The show had already been on for two years, but I hadn't watched it. I really enjoyed watching reality shows, but I never formed strong opinions of people on the shows

I can't believe I didn't get fired for wearing this outfit.

because I didn't know what they were actually like. I definitely like to give people the benefit of the doubt, especially if most of the show is people drunk fighting. I remember feeling awkward, but I tried to show my personality. A few more Zoom meetings and a couple of weeks went by before I got a call saying I was selected to be a new cast member. This is going to sound very Mafia of me, but I knew someone who knew Teresa Giudice's lawyer and they told me to call him for some advice before the show. He told me a lot of people have different strategies but be prepared that they are going to put you in a box. You will either be something like the truth teller, the hot one, the messy one, the funny one, or the villain. I knew deep down that it was going to be hard to fit me in a box, and not just because I'm pear-shaped.

My parents and brother were definitely nervous and worried, but they supported my decision to give it a try. Jordan had gotten the call too, but then he told me that Paige wasn't chosen. I thought it was weird, but then right before filming we heard that she had also been cast. I don't know what made them make that last-minute decision, but it completely changed the trajectory of my life forever. Thank you to the random casting agent who is now either an entertainment executive or hates the industry and became a yoga instructor who does ayahuasca retreats. I have nothing against ayahuasca retreats, but I feel like you shouldn't have to go all the way to Peru and pay someone to give you a drug that makes you puke for an hour, when I can just eat Taco Bell alone in my apartment.

PAIGE'S VERSION

It may have been a chilly day in November, but I was certainly not wearing knee-high boots to my potential new job. A year prior, I had started my infamous Instagram series, Front Paige News, while working as an assistant. I had pitched Front Paige News to the then "it girl" platform and was going in for a meeting that day. This was the first grown-up meeting that I had made happen on my own. I was so nervous, excited, and experiencing true impostor syndrome. The only thing I was truly sure of that morning was what my outfit would be. Earlier that month I had scored a royal-blue velvet pantsuit from Topshop. I was obsessed with it. I later coined it as my "lucky suit" and still have it in the back of my closet. Before I was "Paige and Hannah" I was just Paige from upstate New York who worked as an assistant in New York City, making minimum wage and throwing up in my purse.

I had hit a wall professionally and personally before I met Hannah. I had been an assistant for two years, and the next logical progression in my career was to become a TV producer. But I didn't want that to be my path. I was sick to my stomach. It was the first time in my life I didn't know what the next step would be or what I was working toward. I was partying and living life like any typical twenty-five-year-old in New York City. I had a cheating boyfriend I couldn't seem to quit and a job I couldn't imagine having for the next three minutes let alone the next thirty years. Although it was a steady job with a boss I loved, I felt completely unsettled. I would tell myself time and time again to be grateful, but I couldn't shake this burning feeling inside my stomach that I was meant for something else, something I couldn't imagine yet. Every day while I sat at my desk, I scrolled and read this one specific media platform and thought about how much I would love to work there. I would watch their videos and laugh at everything they posted. I decided to message one of the founders, pitching myself to them, and to my surprise I was asked to come in for a meeting. I was so proud of myself for even messaging them and taking a chance. Sometimes you don't notice how fearless you can be until it's done. I was going in for a meeting the following week, and the only thing I could think of was *What will I wear?* I had bought a gorgeous blue velvet suit from Topshop and wore it for my twenty-fifth birthday just a few days earlier. It was perfect. I felt like a real-life office Barbie (but in blue).

As I went up the elevator, my nerves seemed to increase and then the doors started to open. All I could think was *Smile, smile, smile!* Greeting me at the door was an even smile-ier girl. I think she may have even been waving. She instantly made me feel comfortable. I don't know what it was and I've never been able to quite explain it, but it felt as if I knew her. As if we were friends from high school who hadn't seen each other in a while. She brought me into the kitchen and told me I could sit there and wait. She quickly disappeared, and I went into my meeting. I was hired as a freelance fashion writer and was so excited to be one step closer to whatever I thought my dream job was.

Fast-forward a few months and I'm on a Zoom call as a potential cast member on *Summer House*. They asked if I knew people named Hannah Berner and Jordan Verroi. I said I loosely knew them but not very well. Hannah and I were now "Instagram friends." She would post something funny, and I would like it. This is an excellent way to make a new friend. It doesn't need to be in a stalker way where you comment on every single post (there are only so many times a person can slay in one calendar year) but to just show common interest . . . and it's truly supporting women in the arts. Making friends is really, really hard, especially in that postcollege, mid-to-late-twenties time when everything is falling apart but coming together at the same exact time. If I could tell twenty-five-year-old Paige anything it would be that God truly removes the people who are not meant for you and blesses you with the people who were made for you.

After not hearing from *Summer House* for months, I assumed I was not chosen for the show. I'm going to be honest, my first feeling was relief. I knew it wasn't right for me, and I would have been completely out of my element (which is usually when the best things happen). It wasn't until the middle of June, when I was in the midst of packing for a trip to Iceland, when I got the call for *Summer House*. I was nervous but excited. It was like I had to be rejected to become comfortable with the idea. Over the next few days I had to decide whether to do the show. I met up with my on-again, off-again-boyfriend. I told him about the opportunity, and what he said to me began to shape my entire career without me even knowing it. He told me he would never see me again if I did that kind of show. I then made a decision that would make it impossible for him and every other ex-boyfriend to *never see me again*. We love a revenge story. The lesson here is to never let a man dictate what you can and cannot do.

*The first beach scene we ever shot on Bravo.
There was a fight going on, so we pretended
to be passionate about kadima.*

GIGGLY SQUAD IS BORN

When we walked into the human cauldron, a.k.a. *Summer House*, we immediately felt safe with each other. We kept searching for each other's eyes whenever something crazy or funny or awkward happened. On the first night of filming season 3 (which was our first season), we jumped into bed like little kids at a sleepover and started whispering about the insane situation we were in. We couldn't stop laughing at the fact that not only were we on a reality TV show but that so much could go wrong. Deep down, we were both relieved that we had each other. The next morning we realized that there were microphones on the back of the headboards so producers could hear everything we were saying. Our first rookie mistake was in the books! The second night, we went to our first group dinner, which was very scary. One of the other cast members started telling us what their first impressions of us were, and their observations and their tone were extremely passive aggressive. We squeezed each other's hands under the table.

Hannah knew how to make light of anything and tell a joke to change the mood, but she was definitely more sensitive and less strategic than Paige. She was the true embodiment of a Labrador retriever, goofy with long unbrushed hair. Paige had grown up going to all-girls schools, so she knew how to handle catty drama and was less scared of confrontation. She was the epitome of a black cat: cute but don't cross her path. She was the yin to Hannah's yang, and they completed each other. For whatever reason, they were brought together to be on reality TV. The moon had to have been in Mercury because it isn't a typical way to become best friends with someone. Trauma bonding is real, and the highs and lows of being on a reality TV show can really bond you. There are definitely easier ways to make friends that require much less therapy, but here we are.

After our first season aired, things were surprisingly good. At a cast party, an editor ran up to us and said how much fun he had cutting up our scenes and how he loved showing our friendship. People were commenting about how they thought we were funny. We started to get people following us on social media commenting about what they saw on the show. To have other people give opinions on your friendships is weird but exciting because we

This is a screenshot from one of our first Insta Lives during Covid. Butter made a cameo.

love attention. We started to get the hang of it. We started becoming "Bravolebrities." Andy Cohen knew our names (or at least knew what we looked like).

We survived and made it to our second season. We felt like we belonged, and we were proud to be a part of the friend group and this insane thing we were calling a job that stressed our families out. When we got to the house on the first day of filming, there was a lot of waiting and a lot of drinking. We had a new energy that first night, because we weren't the new kids on the block anymore. We all sat down for dinner around 8:00 p.m.; we were overlubricated and underfed and excited for the first cast dinner. Immediately someone asked one of the guys a snarky question about how wedding planning was going, and everyone got tense. The new cast looked petrified, and he started to give a speech about his relationship.

Hannah turned to Paige and whispered something along the lines of "Why don't they ask about our wedding?" to which Paige— you know what we're going to say—giggled.

Their world would never be the same. Suddenly his hand slammed the table and told us to shut up. We froze like kids who don't want to get detention. The problem was that once you have the giggles, trying to hold in your giggles is like eating a grape with a fork, it ranges from extremely difficult to impossible. The speech was still going in a very serious tone, and then his fiancée let out a giggle.

He was furious. He yelled, "What, are you hanging out with the giggly squad?"

This made us laugh more. He really did have a way with words. Next thing you know, we were being cursed out and fingers were being pointed and people were saying mean things and the season had begun! The next day, he came to our room and apologized for the things he said. It is interesting how men are very easily forgiven on reality TV. As long as they say sorry, they're washed of all their sins and they're just a guy who made a little mistake but has learned and changed! If a woman says or does the wrong thing on reality TV, she is not always granted that kind of grace.

We started to realize that, at the end of the day, we were just characters in a bigger narrative and we had to hope that they would tell our side.

As the season was about to air, Covid hit. It was equal parts scary, nerve-racking, and also a new normal. Paige was upstate in tropical, beautiful Albany, New York, while Hannah was in Shelter Island with her parents and cats. We were miles apart but feeling the same angst and frustration. Paige was bored with her brother, and Hannah was doing dances on TikTok with her parents. Her dad almost tore his quad when he slipped on a rug during "Blinding Lights" by the Weeknd, and it was worth it. We started FaceTiming and just trying to laugh about this strange, new, upsetting reality that was quarantine. We were FaceTiming for hours, and when we saw people starting to hop on Instagram Live, we decided we should let people in on our conversations.

Giggling on FaceTime is our favorite.

There was not a lot of logic or strategy or any planning involved except that we were depressed and liked attention. We are socially awkward in general, but we really started to miss having community. We did our first Live, and it gave us the hit of dopamine we needed. We were just making each other laugh, and all these hilarious girls were in the comments, and we felt social for the first time in forever. Disclaimer: OG Gigglers are the most anxious and depressed of the Gigglers; please see your physician/therapist! Very quickly, we started to have inside jokes about Paige's brother, Gary, fixing the Wi-Fi and how our archnemesis was John Mayer because he went live at the same time as us. After we were live for an hour, we couldn't wait to do it again. We decided we wanted to go live every single night at ten. We felt a community like we had never felt before. Who were all these people joining these Lives to giggle with us about nothing? We knew what we had to call it. *Giggly Squad*. It felt so right.

Over the next four months, we missed only two nights of *Giggly Squad* (both because of Paige's hangovers). We had a lot of different eras of the OG *Giggly Squad*. The Pear-Bombing Era (where we would get Gigglers to comment with pear emojis on different guys' photos), Zoom-Party Era (where Hannah fell and Paige threw up and broke up with her boyfriend), and Caddy-Daddy Era (when Hannah started dating her future husband). The nightly stream of comments from thousands of Gigglers was the best part. What would we do without them? They would call us out when we messed up, define words we didn't understand, help us think of names we couldn't remember, solve so many mysteries, and unearth some of our secrets too! It feels like a fever dream, TBH.

It all ended when we got the call that they were going to shoot another season of reality TV where we were going to be locked in a house for eight weeks because of Covid restrictions. We weren't able to record Lives during filming. When filming ended, we turned Giggly Squad into a real podcast, a live tour, and our religion.

Us on the poles making our dads proud.

INTERLUDE:

TYPES OF LAUGHTER

THERE ARE MANY DIFFERENT FORMS OF LAUGHTER
and they all help us cope with this meaningless planet. Apparently, there is actual science behind laughter. As the original woman in STEM, Elle Woods, once said, "Exercise gives you endorphins. Endorphins make you happy. Happy people just don't shoot their husbands; they just don't." Laughter increases your intake of oxygen; stimulates your heart, lungs, and muscles; and increases the endorphins that are released by your brain. If we do the girl math, laughter is basically mouth Pilates. The endorphins released through laughter also have pain-relieving properties that can temporarily relieve physical discomfort. It's basically loud Advil. Laughter can also be used strategically to help us out of many awkward situations. It's taken years to perfect the timing, nuance, and variation of our giggle to smooth over the cringiest moment. Laughter is a great form of nonverbal communication to convey humor, bond with people, and create understanding. Also, true intimacy comes from laughing at the same time with someone else.

**OUR FAVORITE TYPES OF LAUGHTER TO USE
IN A VARIETY OF LIFE SITUATIONS:**

- The "he's not funny but his family is rich" laugh
- The "you've been kidnapped and you don't want to get cut up" laugh
- The "your mom is mad but your sibling says something funny" laugh
- The "you're covering up a fart" laugh
- The "your boss is the worst but you don't want to get fired" laugh
- The "your friend is making out with a guy at the bar" laugh
- The "your best friend does something stupid that only you think is funny" laugh
- The "he doesn't text you back but is still watching your Insta stories" laugh
- The "he asks for your Snapchat" laugh
- The "you finally come up with the perfect evil plan to get revenge" laugh
- The "you see a funny meme and air goes out your nose" laugh
- The "you know you're about to ruin his life" laugh

BITS WE ARE COMMITTED TO

02

COMEDY IS AN ESCAPE, NOT FROM TRUTH BUT FROM DESPAIR.

—Christopher Fry

WE HAVE TROUBLE COMMITTING to a lot of things (such as every plan we've ever made), but a bit isn't one of them. Committing to a bit is one of the essential joys in life and truly the glue that keeps our friendship together. We do not do weekly Pilates, make dinner together, or take pottery classes. We do bits.

So what the hell is a bit? There are all kinds of bits, but to us, it's an inside joke or phrase shared between people that's repeated often. Bits in your friendship can feel like your own silly little secret language to find humor in our sometimes harshly mundane existence. To share a bit with someone is special and cute and means that you share the same sense of humor.

Throughout this book there are going to be a lot of bits. We will discuss our old bits and probably come up with some new bits! Life is basically a bunch of naps and girl dinners with bits in between. You didn't think we were going to get so philosophical, did you? And Paige didn't even hit her weed pen yet! (Whenever Paige is stressed, Hannah pretends to hit a weed pen, and that's a bit! Our first bit example!) Wow, writing a book is hard *pretends to hit Paige's weed pen*!!

Humor is our secret sauce. Did the family dinner table conversation get a little too heated? Crack a joke. Feeling awkward on a night out? Make fun of the nearest guy in a backward hat. Our friendship is built on our shared sense of humor, as the best friendships often are. Whether you're going to college, starting a new job, or moving to a new city, finding someone who shares your sense of humor is guaranteed to make the hard days more bearable. We even turned our humor into a career, and now we're writing a book about it. If that doesn't convince you that we commit to bits, then we don't know what will.

We would also argue that if you see life as just a bunch of bits, it can be easier to chase your dreams. Whenever you are scared to do something, stop taking life so seriously—it's just a bit! Want to apply for a job you're unqualified for? That's a silly bit. Want to go up to the hottest guy at the bar and speak in a British accent? That's a multicultural bit. Want to dye your hair platinum blond for thirty dollars at a student hair salon in college? That's just a cute purple-shampoo bit! If you take yourself too seriously, you will be afraid to put yourself out there. Don't worry about failure, embarrassment, or judgment. It's not that serious. When you mess up, your best friend will think it's hysterical.

If you google identity crisis.

Did you know that Hannah got married because of a bit? Yep. When Des first picked up Hannah at the Shelter Island ferry, she complained that she was late because of her dad's golf game. He responded, "At least your parents are alive." Now, this was a particularly dark and risky bit to start off with on a first date, but in his wise, old age, he knew that he did not have time to date someone without the same deranged, sick, dry sense of humor. It was "love at first bit." Hannah immediately started giggling, and that bit still holds strong in their relationship. Whenever Hannah gets upset about anything frivolous, Des is quick to say, "At least your parents are alive." Orphan bits can be romantic too!

After a couple dates, Hannah was ready to test a bit on Des. This bit can be used early in relationships to test a date's sense of humor and overall vibes. You have to make sure that he has paid for some dinners already and then, when it's finally time to buy something cheap like coffee or a slice of pizza or a soda, you look at him with a sweet smile and say, "I got this." When the cashier asks for your card, you give it to them and say in a distressed voice, "He always makes me pay!" and then wait for the reaction. Des passed the test and laughed. If he hadn't gotten the bit, Hannah would be a single mother to a colony of cats right now . . . which actually doesn't sound so bad.

A lot of people ask Hannah, "How did you get engaged?" or "What did you say to get him to propose?" Well, it really was a big bit. Only weeks into the relationship, Des joked that he was going to marry Hannah. So she joked back about what kind of ring she wanted. Every couple days, she would randomly send him links to rings. At first, this was hilarious. It was so out-of-pocket to send a man who you just started dating engagement ring photos, because all those books tell you that men are petrified of being pressured into marriage! Well, that means we have a great bit on our hands, folks! She started with small diamonds, then big diamonds, and eventually got up to the Em Rata double-diamond ring, which he scoffed at! But one day, six months later, he got down on one knee with the perfect princess-cut diamond in platinum prongs and a gold band. Before saying yes, she truly wondered, *Is this a bit?* The truth is that it was. Life is just full of bits, and some involve a prenup.

WARNING, GIRLIES: Bits are a form of manifestation. If you are constantly joking about being broke or messy or forgetful or stupid or ugly, then you can feel stuck in that energy. Self-deprecation is a great bit, but use it sparingly because there are many more bits you can do that don't degrade your true self. If you always joke about being a loser, people might start treating you like one, or, even worse, you might start treating yourself like one. For example, if you make fun of your skiing too much, you could end up with a broken hand (although you could always pretend it was just a bit for content). When in doubt, make fun of toxic tall men, Facebook reels, or your friend's weed pen.

A fun fact is that Hannah and Paige both suffer from—sorry, thrive on—social anxiety. Yes, we are bad at small talk, worse at group dinners, and embarrassingly awkward at being in public for long periods of time. We also panic when given a compliment. It's not that we don't agree with the compliment, but that does not negate the awkward feeling we get when we hear one out in the wild. Compliments, like small talk, can make our anxiety go from zero to one hundred. Our response to the compliment is the bit "Will you please start that rumor?"

So when we do have to go out in the wild, bits are a great way to combat the stress of having to interact like (and with) humans. We can notice something happening in a conversation that will make us laugh, which gets us out of our heads long enough to enjoy a brief moment of giggles. I know some of you are like, "Girlies, you cannot have a podcast that thousands of people listen to where you talk for hours on end and perform onstage *and* claim to have social anxiety." Well, the podcast is our favorite time of the week—we get to take our awkward, scary, upsetting, or boring moments and turn them into bits that we share with each other and you. Those bits act as a kind of armor when we're out onstage too!

For some of our favorite bits, go to page 183.

THE POWER OF BEING

BEING DELULU

03

DOUBT KILLS MORE DREAMS THAN FAILURE EVER WILL.

—Suzy Kassem

LET'S BE HONEST, Giggly Squad is just two "delulu" girls who enable each other by constantly saying "Exactly" back and forth while not really listening. *Delulu* is short for *delusional*, which basically means believing something that isn't true. Through trial and error we figured out that no one knows what is true or not true and everything is made up. Seriously, no one really knows what they are doing, and we are all flailing. Once you understand that, you can start to take over the world. Being delulu is the solulu.

The first step to living your dreams is to start actually believing that you can live your dreams, even when other people tell you that you can't. Those people have no imagination, and they probably have weird eyebrows. Think about it, anyone who says they want to be a famous actor, rock star, or Grand Slam champion is delusional and that's why they succeed. Everyone who has accomplished something great had to start from the beginning when their dream seemed far away and impossible.

But we get it, your delusional dreams still seem super big and scary. That's when you write out your goal and then deconstruct it into smaller, more attainable goals that will lead you there. Your dream can be specific or generic and open to change, as long as it brings you joy.

We highly recommend being delusional in your day-to-day life. The combination of confidence, happiness, and positivity is a mindset that starts with your thoughts, a.k.a., it's all made up. Those thoughts create your reality and your perspective. You can choose to bully yourself or be a delulu icon. For example, when Hannah doesn't fit in her clothes because she ate Chipotle every day for a week, she tells herself that she is bloated from flying two weeks ago and moves on with her day. If you go to a party and have multiple awkward conversations, you leave and tell yourself that no one understands your highbrow sense of humor. Life is not what happens to you, it's how you react to it. Be a delusional queen and one day you will wake up and success will be your reality.

Lastly, never be a buzzkill when it comes to your friend telling you about their delusions. You don't know what they are capable of, and supporting their delulu energy only helps your own delulu energy. If you don't believe in other people's dreams it means deep down you don't believe in yourself and you are projecting your shit onto them. You don't want to be on the wrong side of history, e.g., your friend is starring in a documentary about the amazing company she built and talks about the people who didn't believe in her, a.k.a. you. We support women in the arts!!!

Us on daytime TV converting this guy into a Giggler.

HANNAH'S DELUSIONS

I have been delusional since I can remember. At three years old, I would sit all the adults down and tell them I was their teacher. I could barely recite the alphabet. What a delusional nightmare! At six years old, my dad brought me to an ice skating rink and I saw all the teenagers in the middle doing fancy spins and jumps. I immediately said, "Take me to the middle. I want to do that!" When he told me that I couldn't because I didn't know how, I gave him an evil glare. How dare he not believe in me! At eight years old, I fell in love with tennis and knew that I needed to become a professional tennis player. My parents asked a tennis coach about it and were told that I was starting too late to become a professional. When they relayed that information to me, I cried all day and then made it my mission to prove everyone wrong. I don't know what happened to me in a past life, but I had a serious chip on my shoulder. Chill out and have a Juicy Juice, little Hannah! But that intense delusion got me to play pro tournaments at sixteen years old and a full ride to the University of Wisconsin (go, Badgers!).

After college, I was lost and scared and confused, like an influencer at Fyre Festival or Burning Man. I did fashion internships, cold-calling sales, marketing at a T-shirt company, and was *this close* to becoming a yoga teacher. We always say, you know you are in a dark place when you suddenly feel that your calling is to become a yoga teacher, therapist, or real estate agent. My dream, which I thought was impossible, was to become a sports broadcaster or an actor. I've never taken acting classes, but I did have

The millennial Michelangelo.

Smashing balls has always been my favorite hobby.

Hannah Berner
UWBadgers.com

My eyebrows were cousins, not sisters.

some experience editing and doing some sports broadcasting in college. I came across an old video of myself reporting after a basketball game on YouTube and thought, *Wouldn't it be cool if I could do something with video?* Then a friend mentioned that his company was looking for a comedy video producer, but they required five years' experience. In my delusional brain I thought, *I know how to edit, and I know how to make my friends laugh, so I'm going to apply.* I made a funny video, and they called me in for an interview. I knew I didn't have enough experience on my résumé, so I brought a list of thirty funny video ideas I wanted to make. I felt like no self-respecting experienced person would show up to a job interview pitching work concepts to prove they could do the job, but I was sure that if they saw my ideas and not just the words on my résumé, they could see that I had potential.

Like the delusional humble icon I am, I was hired a couple days later for $300 per week. Now, part of being a delusional humble icon is seeing the big picture and knowing that to be successful you have to start small. This is going to sound meta, but I loved finding myself in difficult situations in my early twenties because I always knew that one day it would make the book that I write about my career that much more interesting.

Also, be warned, delusion will come with haters. Haters are never people who have accomplished what you are trying to do. Haters are people who are projecting their own insecurities onto you. Haters are also famously rational, boring, and not creative. When I quit my marketing job and some people heard I was basically working as an intern at twenty-five years old, they definitely talked shit. I even heard that my former boss told my former co-workers that my situation was "sad." I actually smiled when I heard that because I realized he really thought I didn't know what I was doing. Silly middle-aged white man—delusions are for the girlies! I knew that I just had to get into the video production space and then the sky was the limit. Video production made me happy. Creating made me happy. And I didn't even know it yet but stand-up comedy, podcasting, and interviewing made me really happy.

Admitting to yourself that you are delusional is the first step and quite empowering, might I add (am I British?). Especially as a woman who is trained to take up as little space as possible and make sure everyone else is happy, saying out loud that you want to be a performer or that you want attention is difficult. A woman wanting attention? Annoying. A man wanting attention? Let me get out my notepad, he must have something important to say! For some reason, I was delusional enough to think that my voice deserved to be heard, even though I had no idea how many people would end up relating to my voice.

So I got the job as a freelance video producer, with zero experience. At first, I had no idea how to make funny videos, but after about three months of failing (learning), I had a video go viral. It was filmed by a wedding photographer I met in my flag football league and I wrote, acted in, and edited it. I felt a rush. I knew if I could keep doing this, I was onto something. I was also having fun. I didn't know you could have fun while working. It felt like a cheat code for women in STEM.

I continued to create. I started interviewing celebrities and reality TV personalities, writing my own sketches, and editing everything together. One day, I got a DM from a "producer" who wanted to talk about a reality TV show. He had seen my comedy videos and interviews with Bravolebrities. It was random and possibly sex trafficking, but I was twenty-five with nothing to lose and my brain had only just finished developing, so I called him. Long story short, I was cast on a reality show called *Summer House*. I had never seen the show before, but my bosses were not happy about it. I remember them distinctly saying, "We had higher hopes for you." I guess they thought reality TV cast members were trashy, but I was envisioning the kind of trajectory that Kim Kardashian, Cardi B, Christian Siriano, and Kelly Clarkson had experienced. This could obviously go very terribly wrong, or I could be a Grammy winner one day—all I had to do was learn to sing! But at the very least I would no longer have a nine-to-five boss who was disappointed in me.

Before shooting *Summer House*, I wanted to start a podcast so that whatever happened on TV, people who liked me could hear more about who I actually was. I was starting to meet more celebrities in the office, and I was fascinated by the concept of success

The OG Berning in Hell *artwork when I first discovered Canva.*

and happiness. I wanted to interview people who we look up to about their demons, insecurities, and mental health. Does having a million followers solve all your problems? I was determined to find out. I pitched this podcast idea to the company I was with, and they rejected it. I remember not being fazed by the rejection and thinking, *Okay, well now I'll just do it on my own*. I learned all about podcasting, and I was finding my voice. I felt a weird momentum that this was what I was meant to do, and I was having fun, so—let's keep grinding. I launched my podcast *Berning in Hell*

This is my first ever comedy gig at Carolines in NYC. The club has since shut down, but it wasn't because of me, I don't think.

on my own in November 2018, just a few months after filming my first season of *Summer House*.

But right before my first season of *Summer House* aired, I was fired from my job. At the time, I was surprised and hurt and sad because I loved my job and I thought they loved me, but after writing the last couple paragraphs it makes more sense. Being delusional really helped me cope with getting fired because I took solace in the belief that new doors open when old doors close. My podcast was doing well, and I got an email from Carolines on Broadway, a famous stand-up comedy club in NYC, and they wanted me to do a live podcast show! I was immediately into it. Had I ever done a live show? No. But am I delusional with stuff that excites me? Yes!

The delusion doesn't stop there. I have to credit my friend Michelle Ciciyasvili for this part. We both loved stand-up comedy, and she dared me to do ten minutes of stand-up comedy to start the live podcast. Let's unpack this. I had been writing thousands of tweets that were kind of like parts of jokes, I'd also been writing a lot of sketches, and I had dated a stand-up comedian for a year, so whenever he ejaculated in me, I took his talent, just like in *Space*

Jam (niche reference). I'm joking. Anyhow, like the delusional, iconic, humble princess that I am, I said let's do it. Now, little did I know, the first time you do stand-up comedy should not be ten minutes in front of a sold-out crowd of three hundred people (including family and friends). The first time you do stand-up comedy should be two minutes at an open mic in front of a bunch of strangers and you should do that for five more years and then maybe put ten minutes together. Luckily, I don't like rules or regulations or the patriarchy, so I just did it.

Let me remind you, being a delulu queen does not mean you don't get nervous or feel insecure. I am human, don't forget, even though I have a crazy long torso! I remember before I went onstage immediately feeling nervous that I might have performance anxiety like I sometimes felt on the tennis court. I didn't love competition, and I didn't love the pressure to win all the time. But, this didn't feel like that hell. When I got onstage, I felt a weird calm sensation I'd never felt before. It was like I was talking to my best friends at brunch and there was no winning or losing, I just had to be me. After the show, a ton of people said the stand-up portion in the beginning was their favorite part. My delusional journey was working.

Fast-forward three years to the moment I was ousted from *Summer House* and told that I would never amount to anything. Cast members mocked

This is me practicing my stand-up set at my parents' house during Covid, March 2020. I thought I was going to get back on tour the following week. That was the biggest joke.

me for trying to be a comedian. It's easy to kick a dog when they are down. One guy on the cast once pulled me aside to tell me that he was funnier than me and my career would be nothing without him. I was so confused. I never said I was funnier than anyone else. I just wanted to make people laugh. Fast-forward another three years and I've filmed my first Netflix comedy special, *We Ride at Dawn*! That's pretty fucking delusional of me, but I figured that if boys can do it, why can't I?

Delusion is supposed to have a negative connotation, like calling a woman crazy or too confident. But when you own it, it becomes your superpower. Also, plot twist, if there aren't people hating on your life, you may not be delusional enough!

I also would argue that instead of calling ourselves delusional, we can call ourselves brave. Every time I've bet on myself and done something that scared me, I've always grown. I truly believe that the universe rewards you for being brave. My favorite thing to ask myself when I'm doubting myself is "What if you let your dreams come true?" *overdramatic mic drop*

Women be yapping.

Me when I did the worm in my special taping and my top almost fell off.

DELUSIONAL ICONS

The good news is, we aren't the only ones who have made a career out of our delusions, and you can do it too!

OPRAH: She was raised on a farm, where she would perform plays for the animals, a true woman in the arts. She decided she wanted to be paid to talk, and who doesn't want that? Well, we would actually prefer to get paid to sleep. When she finally got a job as a news reporter she was fired from her job because she was "unfit for television news" and couldn't sever her emotions from her stories. Now she is a household name for her work in journalism. If people know you just from your first name, you fucking made it.

SEINFELD: Today we know Jerry Seinfeld as one of the most successful comedians in the world, but he was actually booed offstage during his first stand-up set. He froze onstage and stood there in silence for thirty seconds before the crowd lost patience and he walked out on the gig. Some people would have taken that as a sign to become an accountant, but he didn't stop performing. He eventually created one of the best sitcoms of all time. Remember network TV?

JIM CARREY: This man is a manifesting king. Early in his career, he wrote himself a ten-million-dollar check dated for Thanksgiving Day 1995. He was a struggling actor but he kept this check in his pocket during every audition. Right before Thanksgiving 1995, he found out he was going to make $10 million on *Dumb and Dumber*. Now that's some witchcraft that even Paige is in awe of.

MICHAEL JORDAN: He is literally the GOAT, but even his talents were not appreciated from the start. His sophomore year he was cut from his high school's varsity basketball team and told he could work on his game on the JV team. Did he go on to practice for ten thousand hours to perfect his craft? Yes. Does that sound like a lot of work and not enough time in bed? Kind of. But he saw something in himself, and that's what matters. Now he makes over two hundred million dollars a year just from his shoes. No, it's not a ballet flat.

ELVIS: Elvis is a king, and he died on the toilet, so we find him extremely relatable. Similarly to Paige being fired from corporate America, Elvis was fired after a music gig because he punched an usher. It wasn't one of his finest moments, but he didn't let it define him. He stopped punching ushers and became the King of Rock and Roll.

BARBARA CORCORAN: She worked twenty different jobs by the age of twenty-three and finally quit her waitressing job to start her own real estate company. Sometimes being a quitter can be a good thing. She borrowed $1,000 and started a real estate company with her boyfriend. Seven years later, he left her for his secretary and told her that she would never succeed without him. Now you can't walk outside in New York without seeing a sign for her real estate empire. She not only decentered men from her life to become a business mogul, but now her ex can't turn on the TV without seeing reruns of *Shark Tank*. A win is a win.

ARIANNA HUFFINGTON: Not only was her book rejected by thirty-six publishers, she also received less than 1 percent of the vote when she ran for governor of California. That's even fewer votes than Kim Kardashian got on *Dancing with the Stars*. Now, her books are bestsellers and she founded one of the most successful news outlets. She also has a net worth of 100 million dollars and her blazer collection is to die for.

VERA WANG: She trained her whole childhood to be an Olympic figure skater but never made the team. Instead of going full-on Tonya Harding on her competition, she pivoted to a new delusion. After being turned down for the role of editor in chief at *Vogue*, she still became a household name in fashion and an actual woman in the arts. Now the men who doubted her have to get married to women wearing Vera Wang's iconic wedding dresses. Imagine making money every time your haters try to get married? Iconic.

MADONNA: After dropping out of college, she got fired from her job at Dunkin' Donuts on the first day. She allegedly got reported for squirting jelly filling on a customer. See you in small-claims court because maybe it was a man who deserved it?? Just because you couldn't make it at Dunkin', doesn't mean you can't make it as one of the most successful recording artists. At the time, they just weren't ready for her jelly. During the 1984 MTV Awards, she had a wardrobe malfunction and her manager said her career was over because her butt was exposed on live TV. Now Hannah gets to use her butt as a prop in brand partnerships and no one thinks twice about it.

STEVEN SPIELBERG: This man was rejected from the University of Southern California's film school three times. He clearly did not know how to pretend to be a rower à la Olivia Jade. He did get accepted by another school but dropped out to pursue directing. He has since won three Oscars, four Golden Globes, and four Emmys, so USC is kicking themselves.

MELANIE PERKINS: After more than one hundred noes from investors for her company Canva, she continued to improve her pitch and learn from her mistakes. Eventually, she founded a $26 billion design startup. When someone (usually a man) shoots down your vision, that doesn't mean it's a bad idea. Without this determined woman, Giggly Squad social media would be struggling. We're addicted to Canva because it makes us feel like graphic designers without all the admin.

ANNA WINTOUR: The devil does wear Prada, although she prefers Chanel. Anna Wintour was fired from her job as a fashion stylist before becoming the editor in chief of *Vogue*. She was told that she would "never understand the American market." She responded by saying it was "character building" and she recommends that everyone get fired because it's a "great learning experience." Now celebrities are refreshing their emails hoping for her approval through an invite to the Met Gala every year. Our invite to the Sleeping Beauties Met Gala is probably just lost in the mail because there is no other theme more fitting for us. Maybe Anna Wintour doesn't see the vision of fur Crocs, and that's understandable.

TRACY SUN: The cofounder of Poshmark was studying to become a neurosurgeon when she realized she wasn't meant to be a woman in STEM. Her first fashion start-up failed, but instead of taking that as a sign to quit, she kept working. Sun has talked about how she has fears and doubts like the rest of us, but she doesn't let her emotions rule her. She is proof that you don't have to have everything figured out right away in order to be successful in the future. This is your sign to finally put that pile of clothes you've been meaning to sell on Poshmark (not sponsored LOL).

The moral of these icons' stories is that big goals take a lot of dedication and admin, but they are achievable. If you do not believe that crazy things can happen, then they never will. So go forth and be delusional about your wildest dreams! We also want to make it clear that we don't believe in toxic positivity. Sometimes we really do suck at things. Sometimes Hannah's outfit is bad, or Paige thinks you shouldn't put frozen foods in the microwave, and we have to be honest with ourselves in these moments. In spite of our imperfections, we believe in ourselves and each other. Confidence is important, and sometimes being a little delusional goes a long way.

Gossiping is how you take down the patriarchy.

PAIGE'S DELUSIONS

Some people would call me delusional, and I would agree. I would add that I am also stupid. Who knew that being a below-average student would help my career? I say this with the purest intentions and self-awareness because I finally understand the saying "ignorance is bliss." If I knew the actual logistics and chances of succeeding and everything it would take to be where I am today, I would have never moved from Albany. However, I had no clue, and I am grateful that I didn't talk myself out of my goals. Sometimes it's good to not know too much or overthink things. You can truly think yourself out of anything. That's why sometimes it's good that the only thing I think about is outfits. What I lack in book smarts, I thrive in self-belief and the thrill of proving people wrong.

When I was younger, I used to sit at the kitchen table while my mom cleaned up after dinner, and she would help me with any last-minute studying or homework that I dreaded doing. I have to preface this story with saying I *hated* school. The entire time. I always wanted to stay home sick and would think of some really innovative ways of getting out of school. One time I put applesauce on my bed and told my mom, "I threw up!" and definitely would not be able to attend school that day. I was convinced she believed me only to find out years later she obviously knew I was lying the whole time but still let me skip school. She truly was the best mom growing up. When she finally told me that she knew, she followed it up with, "I assumed you needed a mental health day and time with me." She nailed it. I needed to bed rot at a young age.

One night I was sitting at the glass kitchen table, like I had done so many nights before. On this particular night I was studying for a fourth-grade science test, a subject I loathed, along with all the other subjects. That same night was the Academy Awards, and the red carpet always started at seven. It was about six thirty, and I kept checking the time hoping my mom would let me be done studying so I could see what all the celebrities were wearing. I'd like to add that I did not have a good grade in this class and should have absolutely been studying, but in the back of my head, I told myself I was never going to need this information and that celebrity red carpets were going to be extremely important for my future and ultimately my career. Delusional? It turns out no it was not. I hosted the *E! News* red carpet for the 2024 People's Choice Awards.

The text I received that glorious day from my mom read like this: "Good morning my beautiful daughter. This is just a reminder to enjoy today. It is truly a dream come true. May God bless you with his love and grace. I know you will shine today, you were meant for this . . . It brings the Oscars night fight over studying to a whole new level."

That text message turned something from my childhood that seemed so routine into a complete full-circle moment. Delusion clearly runs in the bloodline.

I think delusion can come in many different forms: delusion that you really believe that you met your husband at a club at 2:00 a.m. Delusion when you tell your friend you're five minutes away but you're dealing with a bad face day while applying makeup. Delusion that you'll attend plans on Friday that you made Tuesday when you were a completely different person.

One of my more delusional moments was when I convinced my parents that if I moved to NYC I would work in entertainment and actually be able to be successful at it. When I was working as an assistant at ABC News I had an idea for Front Paige News. I honestly don't remember being nervous to start it (which was clearly delusional), but my fear came later, when people started to talk about it. Which seems backward? Wasn't that the outcome I wanted? For people to see it and follow me? So then why did I become so nervous at that moment? I hated working in an office. After my first paycheck I cried to my mom, because there was no possible way I was going to be able to do this for the next thirty years of my life. I genuinely thought my boss had made a mistake and underpaid me. My mom assured me that it was correct and that taxes were taken out. I screamed, "Why is no one talking about how high taxes are?" My mom told me to try reading a book. She absolutely ate with that comment, and I completely agreed. The whole world was talking about taxes, and there began my worst fear of tax evasion. As I was reeling from this revelation I realized I

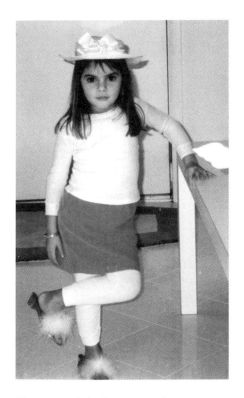

We were ready for the grocery store.

Heatless curls before they were trending.

needed to figure out a way to get out from behind and sometimes under my desk. I started Front Paige News with some of the most delusional energy I've ever had. I prepared five top entertainment news stories of the day to talk about on my Instagram stories. I knew this would only be good and worth watching if I added in more jokes and not just my own opinion. I began editing the videos on my hour after work, and after a few months and incorporating outfit deets, my consistency began to be noticed. Some girls in my office caught wind of me putting myself out there not knowing what could realistically happen. It was then when my delusion shut down and my embarrassment kicked in. There was a brief moment where I thought, *Should I stop? Are they right, am I embarrass-ing myself?* I was so perplexed about what I was actually feeling because I wanted people to see Front Paige News. I wanted them to be talking about it, but as soon as I felt any negativity for it, my anxiety immediately kicked in and that voice of doubt in my head got louder. Where had my delusion gone? When I first started posting, I genuinely didn't think about people I knew seeing it. My delusion was centered on no one I knew seeing it and it being all strangers. I should have been smarter or less delusional, but I am so happy I wasn't. Thankfully I didn't stop. I am so grateful that I didn't because it was no more than a month later that I was asked to be on *Summer House*. One of my favorite things about delusion is that even if you start to lose it, you can always bring yourself right back and focus on being true to yourself.

Obsessed with my mom from birth.

WHAT YOUR NAIL COLOR SAYS ABOUT YOU

WE SPEND A LOT OF TIME on the pod discussing our nail color and the many bad decisions made by Hannah, specifically—she's working on her nail salon boundaries—as well as Paige's inability to move past two shades of pink (if it ain't broke . . .). Nail color, like horoscopes and psychics, can be scary, because it says a lot about who you are. Here's what your nail color says about you:

GREEN (ALSO KNOWN AS GIGGLY GREEN): She's a little rebellious but truth be told she panicked at the nail salon. She is not afraid of looking like a witch and casting evil spells on men. You can go with a darker more emerald green for fall/winter or more of a puke color for spring/summer. Green symbolizes money and growth and not needing a man. This color passes the Bechdel Test.

PINK (LIGHT PINK): She's much, much different from her fraternal twin, hot pink. The light-pink girls are classic girly girls. They have severe anxiety but love a Sephora sale.

HOT PINK: She is self-proclaimed "crazy" and loves to tell stories about her roster. She smells like dry shampoo and loves caramel macchiatos.

ORANGE: She's going through something and will be okay in a couple months.

PURPLE: She loves to say "girly pop" and knows your sun and rising sign just by looking at you. She pulls off a maxi skirt and has a European long-distance boyfriend she met online.

RED: She's fierce, loves gold jewelry, and talks with her hands. She reads actual magazines.

WHITE: Do not trust him with Raquel (ahem, Rachel).

YELLOW: She applied to be a yoga instructor because she's really inspired by Burning Man but then realized she'd actually have to do the course training and decided against it.

SILVER: She shops at vintage stores and knows that she's cooler than you.

GLAZED DOUGHNUT: She listens to Top 40 and has an alarm set on her phone for the next Zara sale.

CHOCOLATE GLAZED DOUGHNUT: She listens to Top 40 and has an alarm set on her phone for the next Aritzia sale.

MANIFESTATION
GONE
WRONG

04

YOU MANIFEST WHAT YOU BELIEVE, NOT WHAT YOU WANT.

—Sonia Ricotti

NOW THAT YOU ARE COMPLETELY DELUSIONAL, you are in the perfect place to manifest. We are kind of obsessed with the idea that your life can improve with the right mindset. Obviously there are many obstacles, opportunities, and random shit life throws at you, but learning about what brings you joy is the first step. Now let's try to manifest.

HANNAH'S METHODS

I really believe in manifestation, but not like "write this one thousand times in your journal and it will come true" kind of manifestation. More like, believe so deep in your gut that you are already what you want to be. It's similar to the idea of happiness. You do not have to chase happiness, it's within you, you just have to find it. This is so Brené Brown coded, let's continue. I like to think of life like it's a single-player game and you want to reach new levels of yourself. You can't just go about your day with no goal and expect things to happen. That's like being a quarterback and wanting to win but not having any plays. Let's get some strategy. I always start big and then get smaller. Write down your biggest goal in the world, such as "winning an Oscar." Then, go backward to each step and write what you need to do to get to that step. *To win an Oscar, I need to be in a successful movie. To be in a successful movie, I need to have acted in other movies. To act in movies, I need a casting agent. To get a casting agent, I have to get a following on social media for*

Warming up before my Netflix
special in my fur Crocs.

acting videos. To get a following on social media, I need to start posting acting videos every day. To post a video every day, I need an acting coach and to write scripts. Okay, now this is something I can start to do tomorrow. If you read this and rolled your eyes and called me delusional: GO BACK TO CHAPTER 3 BECAUSE YOU DIDN'T RETAIN ANYTHING! Sorry for yelling. I realize that every successful person had a time when they had to start from the beginning, and manifesting keeps you focused and calm while working toward a goal. I really feel like we are all leaves in the wind and manifesting gives you direction to put your energy and tell the universe what you want. When you put something into the universe, I don't mean witchcraft, I mean when something is on your mind, you will see more opportunities for it and you will tell people about it. You're planting seeds that can one day grow into your dreams. Farmer girlies, unite! When it starts to feel fun and exciting, that means you are in alignment. If you're not having fun, pivot.

WARNING, GIRLIES: Nothing ever goes according to plan, but trust that you are always moving in the right direction. Keep your eyes wide open and stay on track.

PAIGE'S METHODS

If you've made it this far listening—or, I guess—reading, well, then, good for you! You are officially a woman in STEM. Of course the *M* stands for *manifesting* and let's just say I love a TikTok psychic just as much as the next person, but you know me, I have a tough time believing a single thing they say. The way I like to manifest is extremely Paige coded, and it is another excuse for me to make a list. I like to set a "five-year totally unrealistic goal list." It doesn't have to be long, and it doesn't have to be totally attainable—that is the beauty of manifesting: you can make it whatever you want; it all depends on you and how you feel about yourself, or whatever Brené Brown says. I use these lists as a guide for things I would like to accomplish professionally and personally. I look at it once a month. When I do come across this list amid the hundred other lists on my phone, I fantasize about how it would feel to be living as that version of myself. Now I'm not going to tell you to throw cinnamon through your door on a full moon while Mercury is in the microwave, but I am going to tell you to really, actually fantasize about it. Whenever I'm in the shower, I always feel like I am at my most creative and think of so many things, but as soon as I am out of the shower it's like I forgot everything and am back to reality. Hot girls have short-term memory loss. But that is when I truly manifest what I want.

FIND A PENCIL OR A PEN OR A CHARLOTTE TILBURY PILLOW TALK LIP LINER AND WRITE FIVE THINGS THAT YOU WANT TO MANIFEST FOR YOURSELF:

_____

_____

_____

_____

_____

There are a lot of books (TikToks) about how to manifest, but not a lot of people talk about how manifesting can go wrong. With great manifesting power comes great responsibility. That was a Spider-Man reference. Sometimes we get good at manifesting and then manifest the wrong things and then we find ourselves in a kerfuffle. It's not our fault; we are human, and we don't always know what we really want. Let us tell you our personal manifestation mistakes so you can learn from us—but they may still happen to you because manifestations gone wrong are canon.

My dress was a size too small, and I had nothing the night before. I was in sheer panic mode.

HANNAH—MANIFESTATION GONE TERRIBLY WRONG

I've definitely manifested wrong in my life because the universe likes to keep me on my toes despite my wide feet and calves that could barely fit into a ballet slipper. I manifested a full-ride scholarship to play tennis in college, but I was really depressed and miserable and hated competition. I'd tell myself every day that it made me stronger (Britney Spears voice). After college, I did cold-calling sales because my dad said that if you can survive cold-calling, you can survive anything. I definitely was living by a mentality that I would be successful if I could push through being miserable. Why would I find something I actually enjoy??? Life would be too easy!!! Anyway, I was right out of college and manifested being one of the top sales people at the company within a year. I was making decent money, but I dreaded going to work. I would go to the bathroom like twenty times a day so I didn't have to be making calls. I hated trying to get people to spend money, but that was what I signed up to do. I found myself always talking to the social media team and realized that I would rather take a pay cut and find a more creative role. I quit that sales job because I wasn't on the right path. I didn't want to be a sales manager, and I saw no future there. They key is when you manifest wrong, just switch paths as soon as you feel it in your adorable little gut.

I've also manifested wrong in my personal life. I've definitely manifested the wrong friendships because I thought people were "cool" or "popular" or "fun" but they never really wanted to be my friend in the first place, so it always felt forced and unfulfilling. Once, my mom told me in high school that I should try to be friends with "people who are nice to you." What a crazy concept that we don't prioritize when we are young! I've also had friendships later in life with people who I now realize didn't have anything in common with me, and I'd get caught in situations, parties, and conversations I had no interest in or felt uncomfortable in. The more I would change myself or my opinions for friends to like me, the less I liked myself. Deep, I know. Those are also the friends who are most likely to turn on you or not be there for you when you actually need them. Manifest friends who truly like you for you.

I think this is a canon event, but one of the worst things I manifested when I was younger was finding a successful or famous guy to date. In my mid-twenties, I met a guy on Hinge who had a lot going on, and I really felt cool that he liked me. I hadn't felt important since my tennis days, so I felt like if I was with an "important" guy it would make me feel happy. I was obsessed with him liking me and wanting to be with me. He would tell me things his exes did that he didn't like, and I would take notes in my brain on things not to do so he would never get mad at me. I never shared an opinion that was contrary to his, and my life really started to just be about making sure he was happy. I remember watching a documentary about Dr. Dre where his wife said something along the lines of: *It's his world and I'm living in it. He's the balloon and I'm his rock holding him down.* I did not want to be anybody's rock. I wanted a balanced partnership. I found out later that Dr. Dre's wife filed for divorce.

After almost a year into this relationship, I realized I was miserable. At first I thought I was self-sabotaging because he was the kind of guy who I dreamed about being with and he said he loved me! I started having anxiety attacks because my mind was telling me that this is what I should want but my body was telling me to get the fuck out. I thought I was going to have a nervous breakdown. Little did I know that I just manifested wrong and my gut knew it and had to get me out of the situation. I thought my life would suck if I left him, but it would have sucked if I stayed with him. I had manifested wrong, thinking I wanted to be with a successful person, but I meant to manifest *for me* to become a successful person (cue Cher saying she wants to be a rich man!).

PAIGE—MANIFESTATION GONE TERRIBLY WRONG

Not to make this sound more like a cult than it already is, but I do want to put a disclaimer before my portion of the manifestation chapter: I am a witch. I don't mean that in the literal sense like I'm worshipping the devil and love seeing 666. I also don't mean it in the girl way like *Ugh, I'm such a bitch!* I mean I am psychic. I have deep mystical powers, but the problem is I have no idea what I'm doing; a common theme I think you'll see throughout this literature. For example, I said I loved Armie Hammer and a couple months later the world found out he likes to eat people. Then I confessed that Jonah Hill was my secret crush and shortly after I watched him get exposed with screenshots from his ex that I was too lazy to read. I guess I accidentally manifested the downfall of these men, which, honestly, is iconic.

My mom told me to go to college for broadcast journalism. Her reasoning was classic Kimberly DeSorbo. "You're gorgeous on and off camera and you can read what they write for you." I was seventeen, and I listened to her. I loved my major, and I loved my college experience. She is my mother, and I have been blessed with one who truly does know best. But there always comes a point in adulthood when you suddenly realize that you can no longer ask your mother what to do. At twenty-two I decided to make a list of five things I wanted before I was thirty:

1.

A TV career

2.

Forbes 30 under 30
(before we knew everyone was paying for it)

3.

A big-girl apartment

4.

To be financially stable

5.

To fall in love

I found this list right before I turned twenty-nine. I was so beyond proud of myself. It didn't go exactly as I wrote it out, but it was pretty close. After I got that first paycheck at my nine-to-five, I started Front Paige News. One year into that, I got the call for *Summer House*; three years into that I started *Giggly Squad*. I worked little by little, and I truly envisioned how I would feel when I accomplished all the things on my list.

Sure, manifesting helps, but I can't honestly sit here and tell you that everything I have achieved is because one Sunday morning at the ripe old age of twenty-three I wrote a list (on new, cute, personalized stationery I just bought). There were, of course, other factors at play. My privilege. My parents' help. And a million other things I'll never even be made aware of. I truly think a big part of succeeding is being naive enough to believe you can do things, having ideas of grandeur, having expectations of yourself and speaking them into existence. For example, one time I was on a date—I was eighteen years old and knew absolutely nothing except my address on my fake ID and that chokers were coming back into style. I was sitting on the couch at my date's house when his mom walked in. We got into a casual conversation, and she asked what I was going to do in the future. Without hesitation, I said, "I'm going to be on TV." The funny part about this story is I have absolutely no recollection of it (hot girls with anxiety have memory problems). I was told years later by the guy, who at the time was mortified in front of his mother. He said my confidence was appalling. And then I actually did exactly what I told them I was going to do. I think about that story a lot for a few reasons. One of them being that I love that I don't even remember saying that. It didn't stick with me because I wasn't embarrassed by it. But they were. They were embarrassed for their own reasons. We had such different experiences in that interaction. I love how unfazed I was by my own confidence. I try to channel that confidence a lot more now fourteen years later. And by the way, being on TV was definitely on my list to achieve!

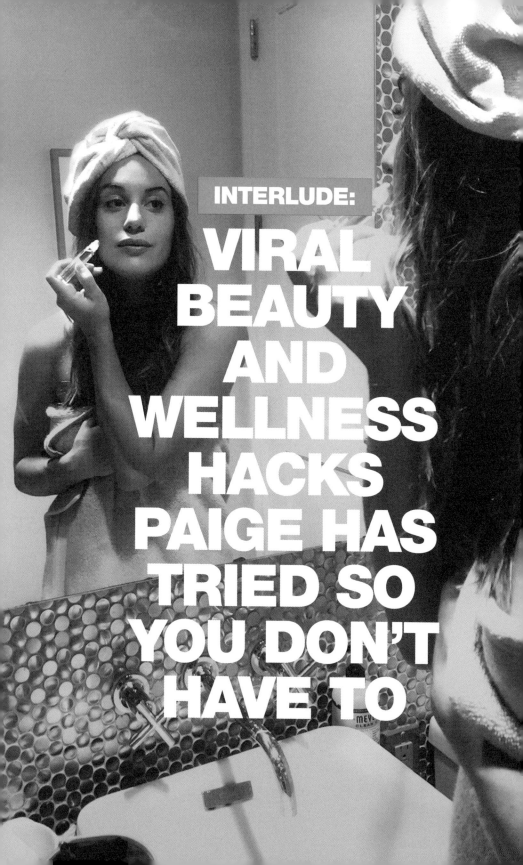

INTERLUDE:

VIRAL BEAUTY AND WELLNESS HACKS PAIGE HAS TRIED SO YOU DON'T HAVE TO

FACIAL LYMPHATIC MASSAGE: It feels good but is crazy expensive and you can just use a $12 gua sha from Amazon in the comfort of your own home. Also they tell you that you have to drink a ton of water afterward, which will make you pee all day, so it's a whole thing.

LIP FILLER: Okay, we've never done this but we know a lot of girls who have and we have an opinion. The consistent feedback is that you shouldn't do too much because filler migrates to other parts of your face and taking filler out is extremely painful—so we are too scared to try this popular trend. Girls like lip flips too, but they said they can't drink from straws, so if that's your passion, definitely reconsider. The turtles are happy.

HYDRAFACIAL: It feels like an octopus is sucking your skin, but also good? It's extremely hydrating if you are like us and haven't had a sip of water since 1996. It is a little more expensive than a normal facial, but they basically use a little vacuum to suck out the dirt and soak a bunch of serums into your pores. We love anything that works and isn't so painful that you wish you had laughing gas *cough* Morpheus8 *cough.*

CASTOR OIL PACK OVERNIGHT (ESPECIALLY ON BEACH VACATIONS): Okay, yes, obviously I learned this on TikTok but can attest to it actually working. Here's what I do:

Make sure you're getting 100 percent castor oil, a heating pad, and a cloth (I use a cotton pillowcase). I put the castor oil on my stomach and use the heating pad for about twenty minutes. I then continue the night with the castor oil covered by the pillowcase. I've been obsessed since the first time I tried it. I looked up everything about castor oil and found out my grandma used to use it for every ailment. It helps with bloating, and I truly think it helps with digestion, but who am I to say? I might be a woman in STEM, but I am not a doctor.

THIRTY SECONDS OF COLD WATER AT THE END OF YOUR SHOWER: I know everyone is obsessed with the cold plunge. But, I've been dunking my head in ice water since senior year of high school, when I saw a makeup YouTube video that said it tightens your pores and makes you glow. I don't know if that's true, but it has become my secret hangover cure. If you don't want to do a whole girl shower, you can just dunk your face in a salad bowl with ice.

HAIR CYCLING: A fancy way of saying you are on the cusp of a depressive episode and feel as though washing your hair has become a ridiculously arduous task. In fairness, I do think there's some truth to it. Excluding hair oils and masks and vitamins and everything else TikTok cons us into, truly training your hair to not get as greasy is an art. My ideal week is:

SUNDAY:
Girl shower, blow out

MONDAY:
Luxurious hair

TUESDAY:
Luxurious curly hair day two

WEDNESDAY:
Slick back

THURSDAY:
Wash because it legitimately hurts

FRIDAY AND SATURDAY:
Free range

This schedule obviously never happens, but a girl can dream.

TONGUE SCRAPING: This is an everyday must. Apparently, if you wake up and immediately drink (even if it's lemon water), then you are swallowing harmful bacteria that could disrupt your gut microbiome. We aren't women in STEM, so we don't know what that means, but we don't like to swallow anything that isn't bottled.

SKIN CYCLING: Not going to lie, skin cycling sometimes induces anxiety, especially when I have messed up the steps and start to spiral! Unless you have a literal PhD and can track what day you are on, this is not for you. The basic rule is don't exfoliate on the same night you use a retinol and that's all you really need to know. If you love routines then:

DAY 1:
Cleanse, exfoliate, toner, moisturizer

DAY 2:
Cleanse, toner, retinol serum, moisturizer

DAY 3:
Cleanse, toner, serum, moisturizer

DAY 4:
Cleanse, toner, serum, moisturizer

The last two days you are repairing and hydrating. Great to pair with your full girl exfoliating shower day.

SNAIL MUCIN: Stop. You'll break out or literally nothing will happen. May the odds be forever in your favor.

SLUGGING: This is a love/hate for me. In the winter and times where you are super dehydrated, I recommend it. This is definitely not an every-night thing. The theory here is after you do your skin care, including moisturizer, you have some type of petroleum jelly to seal it all in. Slugging is not taken lightly here: you *will* go to bed and ruin your silk pillowcase.

PARASITE CLEANSE: I'm actually too scared to try this. I put this in the same box as colonics and enemas. Does anyone really know the difference between the two? Either way, I'm a lady and a tube up my butthole is not ideal.

DIY SPRAY TANS: My coveted spray tan routine is something I have perfected over the years. Of course I have had some utter tragedies, like the time when I was twenty-five and I got a spray tan and cried hysterically because my boyfriend had cheated on me, leaving tear imprints down my face for the next two days. This experience only made me stronger and more powerful, and now I know the tricks of the trade.

Shave, exfoliate, and lotion your entire body. This is controversial because, yes, you need to be fully dry to apply the spray tan but you also need your skin to be at peak moisturization for this to have the best results. After you've moisturized, wait at least an hour for it to fully absorb into your skin. The next step is applying five to seven pumps of Loving Tan onto a mitt for each area and apply all over your body, excluding your neck, face, hands, and feet.

After your body is complete, take a bronzer brush and one pump of tanner and apply to the tops of your feet and hands—blend, blend, blend! Do the same thing for your neck. Take a different bronzer brush and apply Loving Tan Deluxe Face—contouring is optional.

The final and best step is having a big fluffy brush dipped into baby powder or any type of setting powder and brushing your entire body. This will keep you from feeling sticky for the remainder of your spray tan. After you've waited the allotted time (follow instructions), you're ready to rinse. The first rinse is with absolutely no soap or shaving; the second shower is as usual. I like to have my second shower by the time I go to whatever event I need to, but I've also done a two-hour express, not even washed it off, and gotten on a plane. Not every day is a win.

MOUTH TAPE: Don't waste your time, and even if there are benefits to it, my mom has already scared me into thinking I will suffocate myself, so that's a new fear unlocked for all of you to enjoy. If I have to be anxious, so do you.

LED FACE MASK: I have tried so many LED face masks and was absolutely convinced this was a scam and didn't work. Until I bought the Dr. Dennis Gross LED mask and it truly did change the brightness of my skin.

MAGNESIUM FOR SLEEP: The infamous sleepy-time drink made popular by TikTok may actually have something to it. Different from melatonin, there are no loopy dreams, no hangover in the morning, and it ultimately doesn't make you feel like you were hit by a bus.

MELATONIN: If you're looking to run from your problems and develop a drug addiction to something that can be packaged like a Froot Loop box then absolutely be my guest. I will say it is good to have on hand for those nights you'll try anything. Fun fact: one of my friends accidentally gave her daughter a melatonin addiction—the problem was ultimately rectified—but moving forward melatonin should be added to the D.A.R.E. program. And we all remember when Hannah tried it—her mother didn't hear from her for thirty-six hours and almost called the police, therefore Giggly Squad cannot condone its use.

DERMAPLANING: What clean-aesthetic girlies call "shaving your face." I unfortunately missed the dermaplaning era because I immediately lasered my face as soon as lasering was invented. Dermaplaning for those who don't know is a very thin razor that gets rid of peach fuzz and is supposed to help with acne scars and overall appearance of skin.

SKIN CARE MINI FRIDGES: I know these could not be more Paige coded, but I have actually never owned one. I do, however, have a bin in my refrigerator dedicated to skin care. Putting under-eye patches, face masks, gua sha, jade, and ice rollers in the refrigerator add a spa-like element. Keeping one on your vanity is adorable in theory, but I hate clutter, and New York City is too tight for space.

FULL GIRL-SHOWER ROUTINE: Girl showering has become something I can't live without, but only once a week because honestly it's a lot of admin. So many girls complain about their men watching football on Sunday—I say praise be because you need a minute to yourself. I like to start mine by oiling my hair. I do this about an hour before my shower to really let it soak in. Rosemary oil is my favorite, but whatever is currently trending, I will try. The most important part of hair oiling is really massaging it into your head. I like to designate a brush just for hair oiling that feels extra good on my scalp. After that is complete, I like to dry brush. Now I don't remember to do this all the time, but I feel like trying it at least three times counts. While in the shower I like to exfoliate, shave, and oil. After I've made myself a literal seal, I like to pour oil on my entire body and rub it in. Rinse off a little and dry off. I immediately apply an array of different moisturizers but my tried-and-true, if I am really dry, is Aquaphor mixed with some type of moisturizer. My favorite brand is Nécessaire because it is clean and our skin is our biggest organ! After I've completely hydrated, I do my face skin care routine and my hair care. Sometimes I will do a hair mask and rinse it out in the morning or give myself a blowout to start the week. I end with my Dr. Dennis Gross LED mask and put on a cute pajama set. A pajama set can change your entire outlook on life. I truly believe that if more men in politics wore pajama sets they would be less angry.

Pretending I'm zen while shooting reality TV.

HIGH-
FUNCTIONING
ANXIOUS
GIRLIES

05

IF YOU CAN DANCE AND BE FREE AND NOT BE EMBARRASSED YOU CAN RULE THE WORLD.

—Amy Poehler

WE ARE SELF-PROCLAIMED, self-diagnosed, and self-obsessed socially anxious girls! It's not our fault, and it doesn't define who we are. It makes us funny, relatable, and human. If we are going to blame someone for our anxiety, it would probably be our Italian ancestors who immigrated to America, and that sounds pretty stressful, and apparently it got passed on through our DNA because we are women in STEM, so we literally had no chance of being chill. In the twentieth century, when women had anxiety or anger, or were "too emotional," they were called hysterical, put into sanatoriums, and/or forced to get lobotomies. Nowadays, we just harness that emotion into a good podcast episode, because we are women in the arts. We are multifaceted beings with a wide range of emotions, and as we've gotten older, we've learned how to embrace our emotions, fears, and anxieties. Once you stop letting your anxiety control you, the world is your oyster and you don't need to get a lobotomy (even though that does sound quite peaceful).

HANNAH'S ANXIETY

I actually didn't know I had anxiety until I was in my mid-twenties, which is hilarious because I used to call my mom and ask her not to let me go to parties. It wasn't until I'd experienced a couple mental breakdowns in my twenties that I realized I needed to talk to a therapist. She helped me understand that the voices I was hearing in my head weren't actually me. These negative voices were from bad experiences in my past, almost like having a toxic roommate living in your brain constantly telling you that you're not good enough and reminding you of everything that can possibly go wrong or getting stuck in regrets from the past. Once I realized that I didn't have to listen to these voices, it felt like a life hack. When you choose to ignore the voices and be compassionate and nice to yourself instead, a weight gets lifted. Being mean to yourself does not help you, and you don't deserve it. When I realized that I could mess up and not beat myself up about it, everything became easier. I also went on Prozac to help shut up the voices even more because sometimes those bitches are persuasive!

Aside from going to therapy, I like to call my mom, a friend, or an emotionally intelligent man in my life to voice my fears. Something about saying what I'm stressed about out loud makes it less scary—and when it doesn't feel like a bad secret I'm hiding, it loses its power. Another person can help you logically talk about a fear so that you can put it to bed. For example, if I had an awkward interaction with my boss at work that I can't stop hyperfixating on and cringing about, I will tell it to my friend, and they will help me laugh about it or feel less alone. I'm especially bad with this in social situations. I'm annoying and call myself an "empath" but I think I'm just a people pleaser who is obsessed with people around me having a good time and liking me. If I feel like a social interaction didn't go well, I get really down and mad at myself and blame myself for being weird. Most of the time, the other person probably leaves the conversation thinking they were the weird one or even, more likely, they enjoyed the conversation and they DON'T THINK ABOUT THE INTERACTION EVER AGAIN. How freeing that must be. Once, I had a girl come up to me and apologize for a comment she made to me a couple months ago about my dress that she thought might have come off rude and I had no recollection. I actually really liked the girl and was upset the interaction caused her any stress. We are all silly idiots!

Sometimes you have weird social moments because you simply don't vibe with another person's energy, no matter what you bring to the conversation. The interaction feels like oil and water (a reference for the women in STEM). There are eight billion people in the world, so you can move on and have awkward small talk with someone else. My advice when it comes to small talk is similar to how I approach crowd work at a stand-up comedy show . . . just say what you think everyone is thinking and if it bombs, they don't really get you, and if it crushes, then you have a new friend. This typically involves me being in the corner, saying something along the lines of "Are we cool enough to be here?" or "Is this supposed to be fun?" The right people will gravitate toward your strange energy. If you try too hard to be something you're not, you will attract the wrong people and be forced to talk about politics or the architecture of the building or something else boring as fuck.

Over time I've learned that I don't enjoy large groups, parades, big dinners, or parties in general. At first I thought that something was wrong with me, but I learned that I can only be in those situations in small doses because it drains my social battery fast. I learned that I actually thrive in one-on-one conversations or if I have a microphone alone onstage—and that's okay! I spent so much time in my twenties being miserable, trying to enjoy a party with a pit in my stomach. Once I realized that I don't have to do what other people consider "fun," I started being happier. The hardest part of my twenties was thinking something was off with me because everyone else liked to "party," but I didn't understand why we were celebrating and I didn't love alcohol. Little did I know, in your thirties most people settle down a little and a nice one-on-one brunch after going to bed early the night before is considered "chic."

I would have probably enjoyed parties more if I partook in alcohol and drugs. I drank, but I wasn't very good at it and would eventually get sleepy or just slurry or just start beer farting on the dance floor and blaming the guy next to me. I smoked a little weed in high school, but it heightened my anxiety because I thought that my brain broke. It made me even more annoying and paranoid. I once sat on an ottoman and freaked out because there wasn't anywhere to rest my back. It wasn't my best work. My favorite was when I took one hit and then went to the bathroom and looked in the mirror perplexed for thirty minutes about whether my face was round or oval. I once snorted a bump of cocaine and immediately got a nosebleed. It's embarrassing. I also discovered that melatonin is a hell of a drug. I recently took it for the first time and slept for thirty-six hours and my mom almost called the police. I can barely handle a whole-milk iced latte without losing my cool and shitting my pants. Living in the fast lane can be difficult!

For some reason, when bad things happen to me, my favorite hobby is to catastrophize—like no one in this world has ever experienced something this bad and I will never be able to move past it. Now that I've become aware that I catastrophize (I know, it's a big word), I'm able to label it and detach from it. But the key to overcoming hard times (pretty much the entire premise of this book and the only thing we hope you take from it), is to not take life so seriously. Once I realized that I can choose how to respond to situations, I regained control. I obviously cannot control the future (no matter how many psychics I'm DMing on Instagram at any given moment), but I can control how I react to it. I never fully understood when people would say "Choose happiness," like, it's not that fucking easy. But then I realized that the world does respond to your energy. If you are constantly seeing the glass half empty and have a "woe is me" mentality, the universe flows in that direction. If bad things happen to you and you find the funny in it, that positivity really helps you stay afloat. In order to be successful, you have to fail your way to the top. If a couple failures makes you depressed, you will stay failing. If you stay positive, you will fail forward so many times that you will look back at your life and be so thankful that you didn't give up on yourself. For example, if you get broken up with, you can laugh about how it happened and how he reminded you too much of your dad anyway. On the other hand, you can tell yourself that no one will ever love you and he was your last chance at happiness. Only you can control how you frame things and your reactions, and even if you want to be negative, remember that it's just your anxiety talking and we don't trust that bitch.

UPDATE: Okay, when I wrote that last paragraph, I was still a month away from shooting my Netflix special. I was cool as a cucumber. I was confident and doing multiple shows a week and loving all my material. It almost seemed like a fever dream. *Could it really be this easy? Could things just go well for me? Do I deserve this?* The voices started to whisper in my head. But, because I have no clue how to process an emotion, I pushed them down. Two weeks before my special, I got offstage and I had an onslaught of nerves. *This taping could be my only chance. This filmed performance can make or break my entire career.* The voices were getting quite chatty at this point. I woke up the next morning with a jolt. Now, if you know me, I never wake up with a jolt. I will press snooze six times and then scroll on my phone and only get up when I have to pee, and then I still might go back to bed. My heart was pounding, and my mind was racing. I got scared. I'd like to blame 9/11 or at least the MySpace Top 8 for my anxiety, but regardless, my demons were full throttle, and I didn't know where they came from. I dealt with a lot of performance anxiety when I played tennis, and I would choke all the time. I put a ton of pressure on myself and got really good at doubting myself in important moments. I wanted to win so badly that I would lose. I hated that side of me. If I lost, I was so ashamed and really didn't feel lovable or adorable or cunty at all. I was worthless.

But comedy was different. It wasn't a sport. It was a healthy expression of joy. It was an art form. Laughter literally fixes trauma! It has been the safe space where I feel completely myself and feel no pressure! However, for the first time in my career, I felt those old tennis voices coming back. *You aren't good enough. You will fuck this up. Everyone is going to be disappointed in you.* I really thought this old Hannah couldn't come to the phone because she's dead à la Taylor Swift, but this bitch was back and would not shut the fuck up. The more I tried to get the voices to stop, the louder they would get. I started to feel embarrassed and ashamed. *Why am I so weak? Why can't I make it stop? Have I lost my mind? What was I like when I was chill?*

I called Des, and you know when you start the conversation like you're fine and then they ask you what's going on and then you start crying? It basically went like:

DES:

Hey!

ME:

Hey!

DES:

I'm leaving the gym and about to get some coffee.

ME:

Nice! How was your workout?

DES:

Good, my knee is feeling better.
How are you doing?

ME:

(bursts into tears) I'm kind of freaking out right now.

DES:

Wait, what?

ME:

I'm feeling nervous about the special, and I can't
get the nerves to stop.

DES:

(starts laughing hysterically)
Finally, you were way too calm and it was worrying me.

The cool thing about being married to another comedian, who has shot many specials before, is that he was able to give me some perspective. He basically told me that my emotions were perfectly normal. That it is important to feel the weight of the moment and not hold it in. He said this is how all comics feel before a big performance. He calmed me down, but then I texted my therapist who I had broken up with six months ago because I was "feeling great."

She told me to get the energy out, to push hard against a wall. It actually felt amazing. I had so many pent-up feelings that I was scared to face. She told me to cry. That was awkward. Then she told me to visualize breathing in bright blue light and then blow out gray smoke. I was confused, but it did feel nice. Then she told me to dance to a song but make sure that I'm off rhythm so I have to focus on my movements. That was really awkward, but I was desperate at this point. She could have told me to bleach my eyebrows and bark like a dog and I would have done it if it meant I would calm the fuck down. Finally, she asked me what music I like to listen to during shows. I said that I like "Princess Diana" by Ice Spice and Nicki Minaj. She told me to sing it to her. I was like, "Um, it's not really that kind of song." She was like, "Don't worry, you can pull up the lyrics and just sing them to me." I was not looking forward to rapping "grahhh" to my therapist. How did I get myself in this position? But I was desperate, so on Zoom, to my therapist, I rapped the lyrics that went on three minutes too long that included "When we come out, it look like Princess Diana on the street, graah . . . "

Fast-forward two weeks later, I was about to step onstage. The moment before they announced my name, I felt a weird sense of calm come over me. I could do this. I was prepared, and I love what I do. *What if I let my dreams come true?* Both shows could not have gone better. Even though my demons tried to repeat history and ruin the party, I was not the same scared teenager on a tennis court. I had done a lot of work on myself and I believed in myself, and I didn't let the voices win. We are going to feel anxious when we challenge ourselves and try to accomplish hard things. We are human, and that's what makes life interesting. As zaddy Robert Frost said, "I can see no way out but through." Feel your feelings, embrace them, and you will get through it. During this time, the Gigglers were sending me messages of support every day and telling me how they cope with their anxiety. And they sent a lasagna to the green room the night of the filming. If that isn't girlhood, I don't know what is.

PAIGE'S ANXIETY

I had always been an anxious person, even before I knew what anxiety was. Every August before the school year would start, I would get these horrible stomach aches. I'd be emotional or throw temper tantrums. My mom started to pick up on the pattern that I could feel the dreaded school year looming and I would act out because of pure panic to start a new grade. As I continued to get older my anxiety started to show up in a physical sense. I would get nauseous before any group event in high school and that only got worse once college started. Through all of this it wasn't until I was thirty-one that I ever experienced a true hit-you-in-the-face panic attack.

Hannah and I had just started our second national tour, and I was coming off the heels of filming my seventh season of *Summer House*. Anxiety was already high, and it was settling in that I had just begun a fifty-two city, sixty-five show tour, with no end in sight. The thing about panic attacks is sometimes you have no idea what your triggers even are or what is causing you to panic. All that was running through my mind was that I had done a tour before so how could I possibly be this nervous.

Let me start with how our day began. We landed in Denver, excited to get to the hotel because I preemptively made IV appointments for Hannah and I. In reality, Grace made the appointments. When we started our appointments, Hannah and I were immediately laughing at the absurdity of us calling a nurse to our hotel. Our nurse said she had to stop my IV and switch needles. When I asked if something was wrong, she said "Oh no, your veins are just so small that I need a thinner needle." I immediately locked eyes with Hannah because I knew she would have a witty rebuttal. She piped up and said, "What about my veins? Do they need the child size needles as well?" The nurse quickly responded with a swift "No," and Hannah and I burst out into belly laughs. I even looked at Hannah at one point and said "See? Isn't getting an IV fun?" Oh how wrong I would be. ...

After my IV was all set and working correctly, I was talked into adding NAD to my IV. I had no idea what NAD was. All I knew was that Hailey Bieber does it, so I absolutely needed to try it. As soon as she added it to my IV pack, I started to panic. Why had I just agreed to add something I didn't know about to a plastic bag connected to an IV going directly into my bloodstream. My mom's voice started going off like alarm bells in my brain. This nurse could have literally added anything to this IV drip, and, worst of all, I'd asked her to. I looked to my right while all of this sheer panic was going through my head and saw a calm-as-could-be Hannah eating my left-over chicken fingers and fries. At this point the NAD was making me nauseous and drowsy. The nurse assured me it would wear off in ten minutes. I was staying hopeful and trying not to freak out. Grace has been staring at me for twenty-five minutes, and, at this point, she knew I was trying to keep it together. The IV was complete, and I was starting to feel a little bit back to normal despite the altitude and additional factors that were completely unnecessary—like an antiaging drug a supermodel talked about one time.

The makeup artist, Madeline, arrived, and she was truly an angel sent from heaven. We got to talking, and I told her that at the last show I was dealing with some stage fright that I could not shake. It was in that moment that Madeleine changed my whole life. She asked if I had ever taken a beta-blocker. I had never even heard of them. She said a friend of hers had some and that she could stop over and get one before the show. I still wasn't convinced I really needed it until I saw Hannah nod to Madeline agreeing that she should pick one up.

That night, when we got to the venue, it wasn't until a good twenty-five minutes into me deep breathing that my impostor syndrome started to win. Thoughts were running through my head like *I don't deserve to be on that stage and I can't do it*. It was not a time for rational thoughts. As I was holding my hair with one hand and dry heaving in the other, I started to hear spa music coming from Hannah's phone. I loved the effort, but I could not focus enough to tell her I was going to rip my hair out.

My first thought was to call my mom thinking that she would surely comfort me. When she picked up my FaceTime, I was met with her and my dad's faces telling me to calm down and get a hold of myself. I know their type of comfort, and my mom thinks if she makes a big deal of something that I will follow suit. I was trying to listen to her and to get a hold of myself, but my hands were going numb and something more physical was starting to take place. I hung up from my parents, and I asked Grace to get our agent who happened to be sitting in the crowd. I was fully prepared to tell him I could not go out on stage because I thought I was dying and needed an ambulance. In the thirty seconds between when I hung up from my mom and asked Grace to get Andrew from the crowd, Madeline had walked in with the beta-blockers. I took one, but, by that point, tears were already streaming down my face. I walked into the hallway, took a few deep breaths and slowly started to breathe at a regular pace. Hannah opened the door to the hallway at the perfect time, and I said if I don't go now, I'll never be able to do it. As we walked out on-stage Hannah told me I didn't have to talk at all. I could just sit there, and she would have my back. I knew that I had to actually speak words when I got out there, but knowing I had the security blanket Hannah was offering to me, helped me get through the show. As soon as the microphone was in my hand, I immediately told the Gigglers what had transpired in the forty-five minutes we were backstage. Even managing to joke about veins being Hannah- or Paige-coded.

Three shows later and finding underground beta-blockers from anyone I could think to ask, I was back in New York. I immediately called my doctor for a beta-blocker prescription. I had never been so thankful for Daphne and these little orange pills.

Mid–panic attack piccy.

WHAT YOUR PET SAYS ABOUT YOU

THERE IS A THEORY THAT PEOPLE LOOK LIKE THEIR pets. Hannah believes she birthed Butter, so of course they resemble each other (they both look like Cindy Crawford). Paige would love to claim her parents' dog Polo as her own, but it's impossible because he is literally blond and doesn't have long beautiful fingers with a French manicure. However, we think the kind of pet you have says a lot about who you are at your core.

BLACK CAT: You love the "leave at the door" option on Uber Eats so that you never come in contact with other living things and can rot in bed if you desire. You always look like you are pissed off, and that's because you are. You never respond in the group chat, and you've never posted a caption that was more than four words.

ORANGE CAT: You love attention and being the life of the party. You are the only one who has the confidence to grab the aux cord and start DJing in the Uber. You're known for ruining group photos with your "silly face," and you love FaceTiming everyone all the time, even when you have nothing to say.

CALICO CAT: You are the most interesting friend to look at. You know you're beautiful, but you also like being different. You pull off ear cuffs and stick-and-poke tattoos. Sometimes people are jealous of you, but your mom told you that would happen.

PITBULL: You look tough but you are actually just a big teddy bear. You will start a fight with your boyfriend because you're bored, but if it gets too heated you will cry. You have a little social anxiety with big groups of people, so sometimes you drink too much at the pregame and pass out before the bar.

RESCUE MUTT: You tell everyone you're an "empath" and hate designer labels. You shop at Goodwill and make your own toothpaste. It's the first thing you bring up in conversations. You shop at Trader Joe's when you aren't making sourdough bread from scratch.

POMERANIAN: You are always perfectly groomed with your nails done, bows in your hair, and laminated brows. You act like your "shit don't stink." Unfortunately, you have crippling anxiety and never leave your house. You are really good at Facetune and post a ton of selfies that get a ton of likes.

LABRADOODLE: You listen to Top 40 music and strictly wear Zara, Lululemon, and Aritzia. Every fall you make sure that everyone knows how excited you are to drink pumpkin spice lattes. You love the harvest bowl at Sweetgreen, and before the pandemic you never missed a week of SoulCycle.

HUSKY: You love the outdoors, and your family runs a 5K on Thanksgiving. You grew up skiing, and you love to go hiking to "clear your mind." You always have a granola bar in your bag. You don't wear a lot of makeup because you have incredible cheekbones.

FRENCH BULLDOG: You had side bangs and bad eyebrows in high school, and you love showing people photos of it. You go to Equinox to stretch and flirt with finance bros. You got lip filler even though your boyfriend said you didn't need it. You have an addiction to buying fake bags on dhgate.com.

GOLDEN RETRIEVER: You use your Dyson Airwrap every morning because you're perfect. You've never been broken up with, but you still have a relatable charm to you. You keep getting promotions at work even though you have no idea what's going on.

SHIH TZU: You will not stop telling everyone how you could have been a gymnast if you hadn't sprained your knee in third grade. You love hot-girl walks and Adderall.

KING CHARLES: Everyone knows that your great-grandpa invented Corn Pops but you're trying to make a name for yourself. You have your entire wedding Pinterest board planned for an Italian wedding in an ancient castle in Tuscany, but you don't have a boyfriend yet.

GERMAN SHEPHERD: Your dad is a cop and we could never drink at your house in high school.

POODLE: You went to an all-girls high school, and you make it your entire personality. You say you're not high-maintenance, but one time someone asked you to go on a cruise and you broke out into hives.

CHIHUAHUA: You haven't seen your real nails in years. You hook up with all your ex-boyfriends, and you don't think it's toxic. You are always texting or yelling on speakerphone. You are the only one in the family who has told your dad that you hate his new wife.

Some people say that because of her beauty mark,
she is the spitting image of Brooke Shields.

AN ODE TO BUTTER

I'M TEARING UP AS I WRITE THIS BECAUSE SHE WILL never be able to read this. Her little squirrel brain cannot comprehend letters, but she will always comprehend my heart.

If you're rolling your eyes because you "don't like cats," I urge you to stay open-minded. It took me six years to convert Paige into a cat person, and her life has forever changed. Some would call me a cat missionary, trying to connect hot girls with their perfect pet. Similar to women, when cats have boundaries and aren't affectionate to strangers, they are labeled "mean" but they just have self-respect.

If you didn't grow up with cats, you would have only learned about cats from visiting someone else's cat or from the media. I always say that cats have terrible PR. They need to hire someone from the pickleball PR team or Justin Baldoni's because they get so much hate. If you think about it, cats in movies are always in the background, getting pet by an evil villain, bringing bad luck, or running around with a witch. Meanwhile, dogs are a "man's best friend," playing basketball or fighting crime. Now, let me explain that I love dogs too, but I always grew up with cats. Throughout my life we always had amazing cats, including Simba, Cleo, Figaro, Trixie, Clyde, Harry, Willy, and Ragamuffin Ravioli. I have wonderful memories of these beautiful fluff balls cuddling, purring, playing, and loving me throughout the ups and downs of childhood.

When I was twenty-six, I was feeling lost and lonely, and I had just gone through a hard breakup. I was having a bit of a quarter-life crisis. Every day, I would go to work, and when I got home, I'd get under my covers and watch *Vanderpump Rules* to escape my own thoughts and try to feel better knowing that I wasn't being cheated on in the back alley of SUR. I always wanted a cat, but my roommates told me the only cat I could get was a Tamagotchi.

One random day, I got a call from my friend Michelle. She was fostering a kitten, but it wouldn't get out from under the bed. She knew I loved cats and asked if I could come over and check out the situation. When I arrived, the cat came out from under the bed for me, and I placed her on my chest. She immediately started purring. I was convinced she had chosen me. Once a cat chooses you, it's game over. I went back home and couldn't stop thinking about her.

The next day, Michelle called me and said that the cat was back under the bed. I went to visit her again and she came out for me, and we cuddled on the couch. Her eyes were a beautiful amber color that reminded me of Butterscotch. I love food names for cats, so I started to call her Butter.

I begged my roommates to let me adopt her, promising I would take care of everything. Surprisingly, they said yes. My depression seemed to subside as I had this little furry affectionate animal cuddle with me every day. I stopped spiraling about my own problems and started thinking about Butter and how to make sure she was happy. She trusted me and loved doing everything with me. We became so connected, and I was so lucky to have birthed her.

Years later, my life has changed a lot. I no longer have a nine-to-five job, and I'm living with my husband. Butter has been with me through multiple boyfriends and situationships. She was with me through appendicitis, a pandemic, the start of my stand-up career, and the filming of my Netflix special. I sound like a couple on Instagram who hates each other, but we truly have survived so many highs and lows.

The first time Hannah met her goddaughter.

The scariest moment we ever had was when Butter was summering with us in the Hamptons. We were watching someone's dog for the day, and Butter was in her bedroom sleeping. Des and I were playing tennis, and then he went back into the house while I hung outside to scroll on my phone. After twenty minutes, I walked back into the house and immediately heard screaming. My motherly instincts kicked in, and I knew Butter needed me. I sprinted to the bedroom and saw the dog in the room. You never know how you are going to act in emergency situations. My fight or flight kicked in, and I felt like a firefighter. I was going to run into the burning building to save my baby. I blacked out, but Des said I launched my body across the room and put my arm in between the dog and Butter. Apparently, you're not supposed to throw yourself in a dog's mouth; instead, you should pull on the dog's legs, but I was ready to risk it all. Who really needs a left arm? My hand started gushing blood, but, thankfully, Butter was safe. I went to the hospital for my hand.

British accent Fetch me a kitty stick.

I kept crying because her life flashed before my eyes. It was just like her mom to get into fights with boys in the Hamptons, but that event really shook us. We don't babysit dogs anymore, and I never take her safety for granted. I joke that I saved her life that day, but she really saved mine many times before.

I AM AWARE THAT THE MOST DRAMATIC CHAPTER OF THIS BOOK WAS ABOUT MY CAT.

SOCIAL MEDIA

RULES

06

ALWAYS BE A FIRST-RATE VERSION OF YOURSELF, INSTEAD OF A SECOND-RATE VERSION OF SOMEBODY ELSE.

—Judy Garland

IF YOU AREN'T ON SOCIAL MEDIA, congrats on being mentally stable. If you are on social media, it consumes your entire life and you have a serious addiction and you suddenly have the urge to check it right now. Until an apocalypse causes us to live in bunkers with no Wi-Fi, scrolling social media all day is our current reality. As we all know, social media isn't real, so we have to figure out how we want to portray ourselves on social media. Everyone is unique and should express themselves however they like, but here are our tips to navigating social media.

DON'T CRY ON INSTA STORIES TOO MUCH.

HB We don't care what happened. Do not start crying and then decide you should film it. Even if you look gorgeous and rosy-cheeked while you cry, keep those moments to yourself. We think crying is extremely healthy, but when you post it for everyone to see, it seems like you want attention and people who are just looking for funny goat videos are not going to sympathize with you.

PD We are really hoping we don't manifest wrong here but we would never in our lifetime cry on social media—not saying we don't fight the urge sometimes, but after living through reality TV, which is basically drunk Instagram Stories you can't delete, we have learned some moments should stay private, unless of course you're filming and your friend comes from around the corner to scare you and you start crying, then absolutely post that.

DON'T EDIT YOUR PHOTOS TOO MUCH.

HB We love a Paris filter or fixing the lighting, but once you start changing your facial features and body, bad things can happen. If you edit yourself too much, you can start hating yourself in real life. We've heard stories of influencers who will not let anyone post unedited photos of them because they look so different. Obviously, we all want to look our best in photos, but when you change how your body parts look too much, it's giving OnlyFans Frankenstein. Also, if you make an editing mistake and someone calls you out, you won't be able to sleep for months.

PD I have to admit I have 100 percent overedited my photos until I realized the real villain here are the technological advances. No one needs to see their pores in 4K. It's unnatural, and quite frankly there should be some type of fine for when I accidentally catch a glimpse of my crow's-feet. Editing your photos is really only going to make you want to edit them more, and the cycle can be vicious. If you want your pictures to be fun and not have to think about editing them, try a digital camera and it could look like a 2000s Facebook throwback. The moment I realized I was overediting my photos I was so embarrassed.

I've never met her before.

DON'T POST YOUR BOYFRIEND TOO MUCH.

HB   We know it's fun. We love a soft launch and a hard launch, but then chill out. Don't make your significant other your entire personality on social media. The more you post, the more awkward it is when you break up in a couple months. Also, the more you post cute photos of your relationship, the more you have to ask yourself why you want people to see these photos. Do you want people to think you're happy? Do you want to make an ex jealous? Do you wish your relationship was actually the fairy tale that you are pretending it is? Posting your relationship a lot can add pressure to the relationship and seem like you're over-compensating for something. We always say the longer the anniversary caption, the shorter the relationship. Don't post a three-month-anniversary photo with that tall guy you have nothing in common with. You'll thank us later.

PD   It's fun to live in a rom-com and post those cute photos once in a while, but truly keep it at that. Once in a while. I have made this a rule throughout my years of dating, sort of on purpose and sort of that's just how it happened. I had a boyfriend (speaking generally here) in my twenties who, let's just say, did not fit the fucking grid aesthetic. Now I never said this out loud, but I was allowed to have that thought and opinion. When I broke up with him after the 374,602nd reason to end it, I realized I did not need to go through with the very public act of deleting pictures on my Instagram, which would have been so painfully obvious. Why put myself through that, and why feel as though I need to share that just because I have a username? I started to look at my feed as a curation of pretty girl things I liked, and if a man happened to pop up in that, so be it, but I definitely have more shoes on my grid than men.

DON'T BE AFRAID TO FLIRT.

HB Instagram is one of the best dating apps, and people don't talk about it enough. If you see someone in your friend's photo who you think is attractive, don't be afraid to follow them and like three of their photos and then wait. This is an easy and confident way to show someone you are interested without having to come up with anything creative.

PD I've been guilty of unfollowing just to refollow in hopes of getting someone's attention. I have not ever sent the first DM, but I certainly don't mind replying to a story. Black-cat energy comes in hard when it comes to me flirting.

DON'T LEAVE MEAN COMMENTS.

HB Gigglers typically only leave mean comments if they are roasting the hell out of their friend, which is an important part of life. The internet can be a cesspool of hate and pile-ons. Even if there are thousands of comments being mean to a celebrity or an influencer, there is no need to add negativity to these situations. The energy you put out into the world comes right back to you, so use the internet to create and spread positivity. When your friend posts her outfit from the night before, take pride in coming up with the most fire/hilarious/slay/cunty comment to make her smile.

PD Have I left a mean comment? Yes. Have they started it first? Also YES. But that still doesn't make it right. We all have human moments, and maybe one nasty comment is what gets you back into hip-hop yoga, and for that we are grateful. It's okay to lose your temper once in a while, but you certainly don't want your mutuals to accidentally see a mean comment on one of Em Rata's pictures and your thumbnail be staring back at them. New ick unlocked TBH.

DON'T BE AFRAID TO POST.

HB Not all of us are meant to be content creators, but if it's your dream to quit your day job and start hawking dry shampoo on TikTok, you have to post. This sounds obvious, but a lot of people have the potential to be content creators but they are so afraid of starting. To start posting content online is scary because you won't be getting a lot of views and people will judge you. And not just any people, people you know in real life. That first obstacle holds most people back. What will people from my high school think? What if no one cares? What if my videos suck? If you want to get success online, you have to put yourself out there. If you overthink your content, you will never post. Most people who "blow up" online have the same story—they posted a video and had no idea it would gain traction. Enjoy the process of creating (not being a perfectionist) and expressing yourself, and the right people will find you. Followers are attracted to authenticity and people who actually enjoy what they are doing. Who knows what apps will be popular by the time you are reading this book, but to be successful you cannot be afraid to put yourself out there.

PD When I first started posting Front Paige News on Instagram, of course there were about four months that I thought, *This is crazy, this is embarrassing, I can't do this*. I had heard chatter of girls I knew talking about how embarrassing I was for "thinking I would ever get followers or make a career of social media." Of course it hurt my feelings, and the initial moment of embarrassment would make me go into a cold sweat faster than any Zara sale could. I don't know if it was courage or delusion, but I chose to ignore it. Not only did I ignore it, but six months into Front Paige News I started making YouTube videos on the ABC News YouTube page. It was a small blip on the radar, but it gave me such confidence that I wasn't making a fool of myself to the majority of the population. Front Paige News has followed me in my career for years after walking on 68th Street to work. If I had stopped when all of those girls told me to stop, maybe none of this would have happened! What if *Giggly Squad* wasn't what it is? Post whatever you want to post (except crying, obviously)!!

INTERLUDE:

HOW TO
POSE
IN PHOTOS

HANNAH WAS VERY WORRIED about writing this portion of the book until she remembered that we have the number one Limited Too child model in the nation, Paige DeSorbo, here to give us tips.

I know that technically I have been in showbiz and making it all about me since birth, but I truly have been posing for photographs since I could spot a camera lens. Posing is a lot simpler than people make it out to be, and I believe what makes us look horrible in photos is being nervous that we will look horrible in photos! I'm guilty of this too because the number one thing I do when I get nervous or uncomfortable is tense up. That is a sure way to guarantee the photo you just took will look horrible. Relax, it's not going to make or break the internet, so there's really no need to stress.

Once you've relaxed, always think of your posture. I'm always striving for a longer neck in photos, which you create by making sure your shoulders are back and your head is held high. That's half the battle! You've already won if you just stand up straight!

Now figure out your good side. Legend says that your true best friend has the opposite good side as you, ensuring an actual photo shoot every time you get together. Hannah's is left, mine is right. Lean into your good side, have that side always facing the camera. Even if it is a head-on photo, cheat your head a little to that side, angling your chin ever so slightly down.

Next are your angles—you don't need to go crazy, and you don't need to automatically default to hand on the hip. Use what's around you, whether that's a person or a prop. If there is nothing to use and you're showcasing your outfit, walk toward the camera and use natural, slight movements while the camera is clicking.

My top trick to taking the best picture is what you're thinking about while you're taking the picture. I'm not kidding. Look into the camera lens and quickly create who you want people to see when they look at you in that photo. Smizing is something that can naturally happen with your eyes and I'm telling you as soon as you create that confidence in your head, even if only for the second it takes to snap the picture, your natural smize will illuminate.

HOW
TO
FIND
YOUR
PERSONAL
STYLE

07

IMPERFECTION IS BEAUTY, MADNESS IS GENIUS, AND IT'S BETTER TO BE ABSOLUTELY RIDICULOUS THAN ABSOLUTELY BORING.

—Marilyn Monroe

"DID PAIGE APPROVE THIS OUTFIT?" Five words Hannah is, quite frankly, sick of. I never in my wildest dreams thought I would ever hear anyone say that phrase, but I have to tell you how grateful nine-year-old Paige is to hear it. I feel like I could truly write a whole book on personal style and how where you live, what you watched as a child, and society in general impacts our own personal style. The best way I can describe personal style is: You immediately feel different the second you put on an outfit. And by different I mean fabulous, a true expression of yourself. I equate it with the feeling I used to get when I was fifteen and would get excited thinking about all the great outfits I would be able to wear in my twenties. Whenever I get that feeling now, in real time and I'm actually living it, I'm my happiest. When I know I'm in an outfit I would have loved at fifteen, I realize that is my true, personal style. And that can vary across completely different fashion genres. Honestly though, the phrase *personal style* stresses me out sometimes. I feel like it can put you in a box. The box being that every outfit you put on should be impeccable because it represents your personal style. Well, I hate to break it to you, but sometimes I look like total trash, and I like that about myself.

I think personal style is so much bigger than just great outfits. I think it's how you feel in everything you put on your body. Some of my baggiest, ugliest clothes are my favorite, and I want that to be a part of my personal style. Hannah would approve!

Here are some tips I have learned over the years just from being obsessed with clothes.

- Trends will go in and out, and it's fun to try them but know when to let them go.

- Find a pair of jeans and T-shirt that fit and are comfortable and half the battle is done when it comes to putting outfits together.

- Always have a pair of black high-heeled boots.

- Invest in a long, black structured wool coat.

- Have a go with a pair of sneakers.

- If you want to experiment and it's a miss, do it; no one is going to remember it except for you, and there is fun in trying.

- It's okay to dress extra girly, and it's okay to dress in baggy jeans and a hoodie.

Fashion to me is more than looking good and taking a picture. As far back as I can remember I loved my outfits. To me fashion reminds me of my mother. Watching her get dressed and pick out shoes to match her bag. Sitting in front of the TV as a child watching the E! Style channel. Fashion is so many things: self-expression and, at the same time, a sense of community. Bonding with someone over the love of a pair of shoes or a jacket may sound frivolous, but I see it as something that can connect me to other people. My attention to fashion has always been present. I can remember specific dates and times just by remembering what outfit I was wearing. When I was in kindergarten, I would rate my teacher's outfit from one to ten. To her face. I'm sure I was a pleasure to have in class. I would rip out pages in fashion magazines and ask my mom to bring me to the mall so I could re-create the outfits. I think that is why my mom is my biggest fashion icon. I truly learned from watching her get ready. I loved every minute of it. From the moment she got in the bubble bath with a face mask on to the moment she would zip up her four-inch

I cried hysterically after this photo was taken because I was overstimulated.

Looking back, the flower could've been bigger.

high-heeled boots to chaperone my first-grade class field trip to the apple orchard.

I didn't go to college for fashion because I worried that there was no money in fashion, and, to be honest, it intimidated me. I didn't think I could move to NYC for fashion school and pull it off. I often think about that path not taken. Ultimately, I'm happy with the path I chose, but it took time to be able to forgive myself for not being brave enough at seventeen to enroll at FIT.

In high school, I found my inspiration from the early days of Tumblr and Pinterest. *Vogue* was a staple in my household. I would watch celebs on TV, commit the details of their outfits to memory, and try to re-create them from the racks of Forever 21 and Bebe, the only two shoppable stores we had in Albany for teens.

I genuinely believed that every sidewalk was my runway. I quit cheerleading my senior year of high school because I was sick of never being able to pick out an outfit for Friday night football games. I would start brainstorming on Monday for what my "vibe" would be, and by Friday it truly was my Super Bowl fashion show.

QUIZ: IS YOUR STYLE MORE PAIGE OR HANNAH?

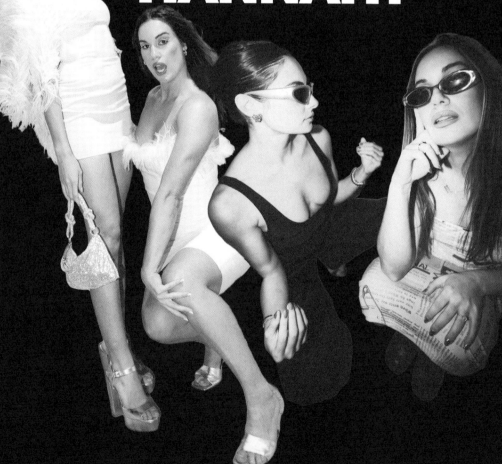

WHOSE STYLE DO YOU HAVE?

Ballet flats	(0 points)
Canadian tuxedo	(2 points)
Tube top	(1 point)
Miu Miu underwear	(0 points)
Granny panties	(1 point)
Zara matching set	(0 points)
Platform sandal	(1 point)
Bows	(0 points)
Oversize vintage tee	(2 points)
DHgate nylon "Prada" with ketchup stains	(3 points)
Chanel	(0 points)
HOKA sneakers	(1 point)
Crop top	(0 points)
Vest	(1 point)
Kitten heel	(0 points)
Navy tie	(2 points)
Capris	(0 points)
Fur Crocs	(3 points)
Cargo pants	(1 point)
Silk pajamas	(0 points)
Midi skirt	(1 point)
Oversize blazer	(0 points)

Seven or more points means you are a Hannah, sorry!!!
Six points or fewer means you are a Paige, congrats! <333

WORKING

OUT

08

IF YOU WANT SOMETHING YOU'VE NEVER HAD, YOU MUST BE WILLING TO DO SOMETHING YOU'VE NEVER DONE.

—Thomas Jefferson

SO THERE HAS BEEN A CONSPIRACY theory going around that working out is good for you. Paige finally caved in and did Pilates four times last month and then called Hannah and said that she did, in fact, feel healthier overall. She also took an edible before that call, so we don't know the validity of her opinion. Apparently, getting out of bed can have some positives, but we are not completely sold. The whole process of getting out of bed itself is a workout. There are arguably a lot of things that are more of a workout than going to the gym, like:

- Having a baby;
- Sending a risky text that your friend helped construct and you don't know if it was the right move and waiting for a response;
- Cleaning your room (*not when your crush is coming over because then you get a weird superpower and you become a human vacuum);
- Getting *the* photo when you go on vacation and you need to post the perfect dump with perfect lighting and perfect caption but look like you didn't try to make it perfect;

- Doing a full girl shower;

- Calling a doctor's office to set up an appointment;

- Convincing your friend not to get back with her ex who likes all of Em Rata's photos;

- Lasering your entire body;

- Getting from the couch to the bed at night after watching nine episodes of *Love Is Blind*;

- Going to USPS and not crying;

- Trying to orgasm when a guy is fingering your inner leg;

- Dyson Airwrapping your hair;

- Getting an IUD;

- Trying to find a purpose in this meaningless life.

But, if you want to start a real fitness routine, we support you. The fitness world can be very intimidating, so we did some research on what kind of workouts fitness influencers are posting about and you can decide for yourself what's best for you.

PILATES: Paige loves it because you can be on your back for a lot of it while wearing a matching set. It's definitely a "hot-girl workout" because you don't really sweat and you can stare at yourself in the mirror the whole time and your slicked-back bun that gives you a migraine looks great. Hannah enjoys Pilates too, but she thinks it is just a socially acceptable form of BDSM. The whips and chains and handcuffs do not seem necessary. Also, WTF is a pelvis and why do they talk about it so much? It sounds made up. They say that there are new muscles you will learn to activate, and it's like, we are in our thirties, if we didn't need them before, why would we need them now? It's giving appendix. Also, your instructor will always be a soft-spoken woman named Aspen with an eight-pack who doesn't eat sugar and loves going on retreats because she hates her husband and children.

HIP-HOP YOGA: Hannah knew she hit rock bottom when she almost decided to become a yoga teacher after a particularly bad breakup in 2017. When she heard how expensive yoga teacher certification was, she feared it was a multilevel marketing scheme. When she heard it was two hundred hours of training, she knew she did not have the attention span. However, she loves taking a particular class that is called Y7 and it's "candlelit," so you sweat out all your demons to the sounds of Nelly. The room is dark and the music is loud, so she can bloat and fart and no one knows it's her. It's quite freeing. Despite not being able to touch her toes because of unresolved trauma in her hips, she enjoys the moving meditation of yoga and fancy words they use for poses. She also lives by the mantra that if you are overwhelmed at any time in life, you can do a child's pose. People look at her funny at the DMV, but she doesn't care.

GYM MEMBERSHIPS: We do need motivation to get to the gym and knowing that money is being taken out of our account that we would rather spend on Starbies could possibly get us to show up. The hardest part of the gym is the process of deciding you are actually going to go to the gym. If we are hungry before the gym, we need to eat, then we need to digest, then you hate your outfit, then it might be too windy outside, and next thing you know, you're on the couch playing Wordle. If you can make it to the gym, it does get easier. You can stress, lift a couple weights while trying not to make awkward eye contact with anyone, and then take some mirror selfies to show everyone that you are the epitome of health and wellness. Not to toot our own horn, but a lot of Gigglers say they listen to our podcast on the treadmill and that the giggles enhance their ab workout.

SPORTS: As you know, we have a sports podcast and we support playing all sports to work out, except skiing, because that sport is pure violence and you will cry the entire time while being frostbitten. Skiing also requires way too many accessories and is extremely expensive for something that is going to ruin your day. We highly recommend tennis because of its cardio benefits, and when you play a game, you can temporarily forget that you are forcing yourself to work out. If tennis is too intimidating, you can try pickleball. Unfortunately you will have to interact with other people, but sometimes you can meet like-minded individuals and maybe make a friend or an acquaintance who will randomly comment fire emojis on your photos for the next five years. Joining a volleyball, soccer, flag football, or kickball league can be very fun if you don't become overly competitive and create enemies for life.

HOT-GIRL WALKING: This is our favorite workout because you can run errands while also getting steps in. Some people like to go on the treadmill and do the 12-3-30 which is walking on the treadmill for 30 minutes at 3 mph and a level 12 incline. This is basically gaslighting us into hiking, but a win is a win. We prefer walking the streets of NYC because we can people-watch and go shopping for things we don't need and call it fitness.

At the end of the day, it's whatever you can do to trick yourself into wanting to move this skin suit we are forced to carry around all day.

Young Hannah didn't go pro in softball because her fingers were too small.

Paige wore kitten heels to play baseball.

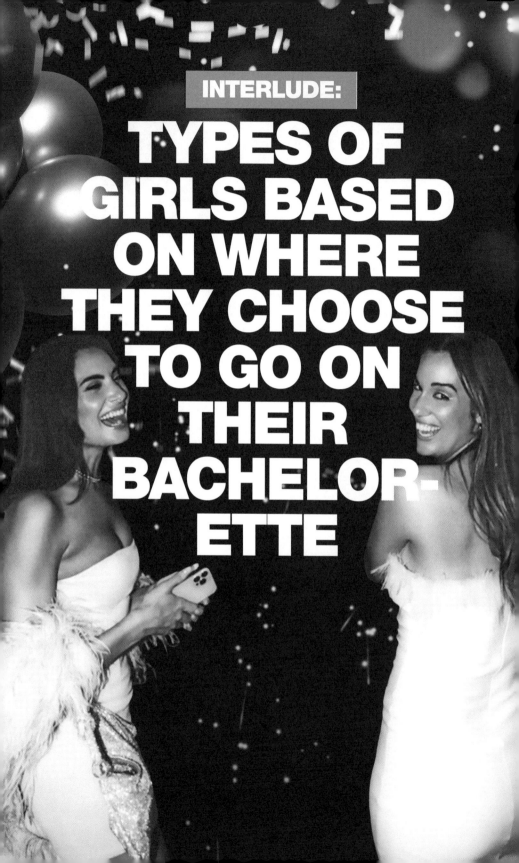

TYPES OF GIRLS BASED ON WHERE THEY CHOOSE TO GO ON THEIR BACHELOR-ETTE

BEING A CULT LEADER, A.K.A. THE BRIDE, requires a lot of admin, especially picking which location to throw your bachelor-ette/human sacrifice party. Hannah actually didn't originally want a bachelorette party, but her friends pushed her to do it. Hannah requested doing something different, like going to an upstate animal sanctuary. Paige immediately vetoed this idea because she would never wear her Versace heels on a donkey farm and commanded the group to ignore Hannah. The rest is history (just ask the Salami Squad) and we have the TikToks to prove it.

HERE IS WHAT YOUR BACHELORETTE LOCATION SAYS ABOUT YOU.

VEGAS: At least three of these girls tried to pursue a career in makeup artistry only to quickly learn that they hate it and want to be hairstylists. At least one has an infinity symbol tattooed on her wrist and has a restraining order against her current boyfriend, who she talks to every night on the phone.

CHARLESTON: They think they are too good for Vegas and claim they want a low-key shopping weekend, but they have been blackout since their last sorority meetup nine days ago. Two of them hate each other but conveniently have the same shoe size, so they make it work for group trips.

NAPA: They've downloaded Duolingo but claim to be enrolled in French classes because they wanted to be able to say the origin and name of each wine. They love J.Crew but would never be seen at an outlet mall. All their dads have had affairs with each other, but it's fine because they paid for the trip.

SCOTTSDALE: These girls are from Jersey. Their best friend is a spray-tan artist who can also bedazzle vaginas, which happens to be the theme of the trip. Brett, the groom, simultaneously found himself on the Vegas bachelorette and his "phone died."

TULUM: These girls have not accepted that college is over or that trying acid for the first time at thirty-four may induce panic attacks. In the morning, they will realize that one of them is pregnant and one of them has joined a cartel.

IBIZA: This is the second-marriage celebration for the most-hated girl in the group who happens to be marrying the richest man any of them have ever met. They all arrive in Dior sandals, carrying sky-blue Birkins filled with Adderall they stole from their children.

MIAMI: These are some reality TV stars who live in NYC and hire a photographer to follow them around. They've hired glam but are too tired to get glam. They claim they are starting Pilates on Monday but have been catching salami in their mouths since Friday. They spent all their money at a club called E11EVEN. Any club with numbers in the title means you will puke in the bathroom.

DISNEY WORLD: These girls were never heard from again to tell their story.

Hannah nervous pooping during her bachelorette.

Club ratting at Kikis.

HOW TO

DECENTER MEN

09

SOME WOMEN CHOOSE TO FOLLOW MEN, AND SOME CHOOSE TO FOLLOW THEIR DREAMS. IF YOU'RE WONDERING WHICH WAY TO GO, REMEMBER THAT YOUR CAREER WILL NEVER WAKE UP AND TELL YOU THAT IT DOESN'T LOVE YOU ANYMORE.

—Lady Gaga

IF YOU ARE ATTRACTED TO MEN, first of all, we are so sorry. Second of all, we have a strategy to cope. It's called "decentering men." It is our religion. Once you start decentering men, a lot of your problems will go away. It's almost like deprogramming someone who was in a cult. Growing up, we don't realize how much of our lives revolve around male validation, male attention, obtaining a man, and even supporting a man. Disney tells us that one day, if we are lucky, our prince will come. Magazines tell us how to dress and act for the male gaze. At family gatherings, people ask more about if we have a boyfriend than about our job. When all your decisions are based around men, you betray yourself. When your biggest goal is to find a man and you believe that will bring you happiness, you feel an insane amount of pressure to meet someone, text the right things, act in the "appropriate" ways, and do anything you can to lock a man down. We love having men around, but we don't need them. Think of them like salt, they can enhance things, but they aren't always necessary and too much may be harmful to your health.

There are so many days that are ruined and time that is wasted because a guy you just met didn't text you back or you went out to a bar and no man approached you. If you shift your perspective to not put "male attention" as the ultimate goal, you will be happier and more emotionally fulfilled in the long run. We will also take this opportunity to shout from the rooftops, *This is hard!* It is a constant practice. Men are quite skilled in being able to ruin your day, but decentering them takes a little of that power away from them. Also, when we say "decenter men," we do not mean to hate or ignore all men. We mean that if you stop making all your decisions based on obtaining a man, you actually will have a better relationship with men and with yourself. You will have space to learn about who you really are and what you really want.

So how do you actually decenter day-to-day? First off, when you are thinking about your plans for the day, think about what activities you want to do that are best for your mental and physical health and happiness. This is a difficult thing to do because hobbies are a conspiracy theory that people just ask you about on dates. But let's try. Do you want to focus on work? Do you want to try a hip-hop yoga class? Do you need to watch a dope documentary? Do you want to hang out with your best friend? Do you want to go on a date? Men are a part of our lives but it's important that they are not the priority or you will lose yourself. If you are choosing what you wear, how you speak, or where you hang out based on men, you will forget what you actually want.

Some would argue that decentering men is a canon event. In our early twenties, it wasn't uncommon for us to change ourselves so that a man might like us. Then once he liked us, we realized we actually didn't like him or the person we had become when we were with him. It's easy to get along with any tall handsome man when you have none of your own opinions. Ultimately, you want a partner who is right for you, and you can only attract the right partner if you are being true to yourself. We've wasted many beautiful weekends because we were upset when a guy (who smells like mango JUUL) didn't text us back. Once you change your perspective and realize that you're not a failure or your day didn't suck because of one guy's inattentiveness, you will find peace. Let's be clear, in five years you won't even remember the name of the guy you thought you would never get over. The patriarchy is structured for you to believe that you are only worthy or happy when a man wants to be with you—but that is a big fat lie. The secret to happiness and worthiness starts with you.

HOW HANNAH DECENTERS

I am guilty of being a boy-crazy bitch. Sometimes I couldn't control what was going on in my career, with my friendships, or my self-esteem, but I could try to control having a cute guy to talk to. I loved having a crush (and still do) because you don't have to face the crippling reality that we don't know why we are alive. There is nothing better than getting a text back from someone new who you don't know anything about. When I'd meet someone new I'd become a creative director and imagine their entire personality (and it's perfect). I'd put on my headphones and play "Hey Daddy (Daddy's Home)" by Usher and envision my new happy life with my new man who probably wouldn't flinch if I got hit by a car. I definitely was addicted to the excitement and dopamine hit of a new guy having interest in me! Now, I'm not telling you this is bad or weird or shameful. It's very normal. However, if you begin making too many decisions around obtaining a man, you will lose yourself. Once I dated a guy who I thought was the *coolest,* so I really didn't want to mess it up.

Us after we cheated to make sure Paige caught my bouquet.

He told me all these things his ex-girlfriends did that he hated, and I made sure to never do those things. Don't make plans when he wants to watch football? Check. Don't make him sleep at my apartment too often? Check. Don't spend too much time with him at his apartment so he won't get sick of me? Check. Wait a second. This guy sucks. Centering my life around him because I liked that he liked me made me hate my life. I couldn't eat or sleep, so you know I was really messed up. I was walking on eggshells all the time, and let's be honest, I'm a bull in a china shop. When I left him, I realized I did everything I could to get the man I thought everyone wanted, and I was miserable. Once I realized that my mental health could be ruined by a man, I stopped seeing them as the ultimate happiness and I started the decentering process.

The first step was watching *Vanderpump Rules*, obviously. When you are going through a dark time, getting lost in other people's problems can be a wonderful thing. After coming home from work, I didn't want to be stuck with my own thoughts, so I would just turn on the show and it felt like I was hanging out with a new friend group and got super invested in their problems. How did Kristen live with the guilt of sleeping with Jax? Is James going to get sober? Are the goat-cheese balls really that good? I was rotting in bed, but I knew it's what I needed at that moment.

Once I could get out of bed, I started hip-hop yoga. There are a bunch of Y7 studios in NYC that have these fun classes and I became obsessed. I'm not flexible, and I don't love working out, but I liked trying something new. It was fun to be bad at something and have no expectations. I was practicing not judging myself and being nice to myself (something I never could do while playing tennis—but that's for another book). When I slowly started to see improvement, I was proud of myself. I was taking time for myself, and it was really more for my mental health. I wasn't doing it for a result or to show off. It was just for me. Doing a moving meditation to misogynistic rap was my shit. I felt like I was having fun with myself again. I became my own (slightly more flexible) best friend. I also started to play tennis again. Tennis was the longest relationship I've ever had. I played it competitively for almost fifteen years, and I missed it. I had forgotten that I had a skill that I was good at, but since I didn't have to put pressure on myself anymore, I could have fun. I could play for me and celebrate this talent that I had worked so hard on for so many years. Back in the day, I played for other people's approval, but now I could play because I wanted to play. Tennis outfits have gotten much cuter too.

I also started to get really motivated with my work. I was a video producer at the time, making funny sketches for social media, and I channeled my dating problems into comedy. Seeing other girls relate to my frustrations made me feel less alone and made me feel like I had a little bit of a purpose. Instead of dreaming about getting with a new guy, I dreamed about the person I could become in this industry. I dreamed about getting my bag. One of my favorite quotes is from Lady Gaga, who once said, "I had a boyfriend who told me I'd never succeed, never be nominated for a Grammy, never have a hit song, and that he hoped I'd fail. I said to him, 'Someday, when we're not together, you won't be able to order a cup of coffee at the fucking deli without hearing or seeing me." It can be fun to use men for motivation or a side revenge storyline.

I have to address the fact that I'm preaching about "decentering men," but I did get married a couple years ago. I still wanted a healthy relationship, but I got to the point in my life that I didn't *need* one. My husband followed me on Instagram because he saw me on a comedian's Insta story. If I hadn't chased my dream of being a stand-up comic, we probably wouldn't have met. On our first date, he was fascinated with my tennis career and we bonded over being raised in New York City. I was being myself because I had taken time to be by myself and really know myself. Whatever happens, I know I always have me.

HOW PAIGE DECENTERS

Not to sound all self-helpy but decentering men truly is at the core of being able to be yourself and be happy without relying on a man's approval. Now of course, we love falling in love, having a partner, blah blah blah blah, but decentering men doesn't mean literally throwing them in the trash (well, maybe). It means being able to take an inventory of how you feel in a situation and what

Can you tell Paige was blackout?

you want. Do you want to go on a date with this man or do you feel bad because he's been talking to himself in your DMs and you're hungry for a free pasta dinner? Now, if it is the latter and truly about the pasta, then we get it; girl, have the best time. But if you find that you don't like the way you act or feel when a guy (any guy and/or a specific guy) is thrown in the mix, then it is time for you to decenter men.

I first realized I needed to truly decenter men when it became clear to me that I was putting their needs before my own in a constant attempt to please them. I started to notice changes in my personality when I liked a guy and how I would conform to things he liked to do and go places he liked to go. When I was twenty-three I had my first real corporate job. I was so excited when I started there, and I was diligent about making a good first impression. It was my first week of work, and my boyfriend had a wedding to attend in Washington, DC. The plan was to leave early Friday afternoon to beat traffic (IDK, whatever guys tell themselves when they get to drive a car). My boyfriend asked me if I could leave work early that day to ensure getting on the road on time. My first instinct was ABSOLUTELY NOT; I just started this job. After much back-and-forth I told him I would ask my boss if I could take the day off. Over the next three days, I was in agony. I was lying to my boyfriend, submitting to what he wanted when I knew in my gut it was irresponsible of me and selfish of him. Finally, on Thursday afternoon I told my boyfriend that my boss said I couldn't have the day off, but the truth was that I never asked. It felt so wrong and entitled to purposely mess up by asking for a day off in my first couple weeks of work. But it didn't matter. I had already betrayed myself and lied to my boyfriend and, more important, to myself.

My boyfriend, let's call him the Wedding Guy (WG), of course lost his mind. He told me it was my fault for not asking sooner and that I was immature and would need to figure out a way to get to the wedding. He told me he was leaving without me and those were my consequences. I cried the entire night. Friday morning came, and as I left for work he texted me that he was going to Washington, DC. I finished my day at work, and as I got to my apartment, WG was calling. My hands shaking, I answered the phone to a stern voice saying I better get on the train first thing in the morning to make it to the wedding. Oh, and he forgot his tux shoes, so I would need to get them before I headed to the train. How convenient! Well, the Scorpio in me wanted revenge, and the immature, insecure twenty-three-year-old wanted to do anything I could to make it up to this man. I never told my mom what happened, so that's how you know how serious things were!

I showed up to Penn Station with a pit in my stomach, knowing I shouldn't get on that train. I stared down at my duffel bag, with his tux shoes poking out of the top. I unzipped the bag, took out the shoes, threw them in the garbage, and then proceeded to get on the train. I don't know why I did it. I've never told anyone that I did that, but there was something empowering in it and also weak. I had a horrible weekend, as you can imagine, and didn't truly understand the severity and impact of how I was being treated.

Now, I didn't tell you this story to stand on a soapbox and preach about how everyone should break up with their boyfriends. It took me years to get out of that relationship, and it wasn't until I was truly scared of losing who I was and, more important, who I wanted to become, that I made a change. Take your time and be nice to yourself; remember decentering men is truly about you and how you want to live your life.

BONUS: WOMEN WHOSE LIVES GOT BETTER WHEN THEY LEFT THEIR HUSBANDS

As if men don't have enough in this world, studies show that marriage is more beneficial for men than women. We swear we didn't make up that study. Disney movies make us think that once we find a man, everything will be perfect. However, typically after marriage, men start making more money and women who have babies tend to make less. Also, male physical health improves due to decreased stress levels, whereas marriage causes more stress for women. If your lower back is hurting, it's because you are carrying the weight of the relationship on your back. Women also tend to not want to have sex because they are so annoyed at having to take care of their husband and pick up his socks. Marriage tends to give men more time to spend on their hobbies because their wife is handling the day-to-day tasks. Women have less time, less of their own money, and sometimes more problems after getting married. As Biggie Smalls once said, "mo' money, mo' problems." We say, "more men, more problems." Statistically, men also get remarried more quickly than women. Going from a bed fit for a king to a single pillow and no headboard is whiplash, so they start the search for another woman to fill the void that is their empty refrigerator.

Obviously marriage can be fulfilling and enriching when it's with the right partner, but if it's not a net positive, being single is way better than having a ball and chain. It's important to point out that some of the most successful and wealthy women aren't married. Oprah, Taylor Swift, Chelsea Handler, and Shonda Rhimes being perfect examples. You don't need a man to do anything because you have everything you need within yourself. Sometimes we have ninety-nine problems and a man is all of them. Get married because you want to add to your life, not because you're trying to make it whole. If he doesn't add value, don't add him to the will. Content creator Drew Afualo once said, "You can tell how much a woman loves herself based on the partner she chooses." We would rather be with no one than with someone who sucks.

The successful women listed below are the blueprint for decentering men. Divorce and breakups are a lot of admin, but these women put in the work to free themselves from the men who were holding them back.

KELLY CLARKSON: She will always be our American Idol. "Since U Been Gone" also needs to be on your breakup playlist. Her ex-husband took over the role as her manager a few years into their marriage. On the surface, we love a supportive king, but it turns out he was not supportive or a king. During their divorce, it was revealed he made some shady deals and owed Kelly $2.6 million. She moved to NYC with her kids to continue *The Kelly Clarkson Show*, which averages around a million daily viewers. She said she won't consider getting married again.

SHAKIRA: She gets double points for this one because she never married her long-term boyfriend who she had two kids with. She recently revealed that during their relationship, she spent years sacrificing her career to support his. We will not be mentioning his name or career because he deprived us of new Shakira music. (Rumor has it the song "Hips Don't Lie" was one of Hannah's favorites for the grind circle at school dances.) The end of their eleven-year relationship started with Jamgate. A rumor started circling the web about how Shakira went full-on FBI mode when she found a jar of strawberry jam open in their refrigerator that someone else ate (see you in small-claims court), and this may have led her to believe that he was having an affair. The fact that women are not running the FBI is beyond us. Regardless of whether Jamgate was real, we love saying the word "Jamgate." Since their public breakup, Shakira has been releasing more music, spending more time on herself, and is earning more money. She also has a significantly higher net worth than her ex, and that must help her sleep better at night. She recently dropped a single where she sings, "You thought you hurt me, but you made me stronger / Women don't cry anymore, they cash in." Damn, this really gets us in the mood to drop $200 at Target for no reason.

MANDY MOORE: She was previously married to Ryan Adams. She has spoken out about the psychological abuse and control she experienced with him. He allegedly discouraged her from pursuing music and chose other women to record songs that they wrote together. This relationship is the perfect example of men sabotaging women because they are jealous of their talent and potential power. If I had a nickel. After their divorce, the show *This Is Us* relaunched her career and she got remarried to a man who supports women in the arts. Phoebe Bridgers wrote a diss track called "Motion Sickness" about Ryan Adams and that is girlhood. If you hate him, so do we. No explanation needed.

KATIE HOLMES: The lore of Katie Holmes and Tom Cruise's relationship runs deep. We all know Tom Cruise is a longtime Scientologist. Shortly after they started dating, Katie Holmes joined Scientology. Throughout their relationship, people noticed Katie's style was changing, and she even admitted she listened to Tom's feedback about her clothing. (Paige is punching the air right now.) She filed for divorce, got primary custody of her daughter, and moved to New York City. Her career soared on Broadway and in movies and television. "I don't have any fear now, I don't have a lot of rules for myself, and I don't take myself that seriously," Holmes told *People* in October 2014. "I feel ready for new challenges." We ride at dawn!

WRITE DOWN TEN THINGS YOU ENJOY THAT DON'T HAVE ANYTHING TO DO WITH THE MALE SPECIES.

1. _____
2. _____
3. _____
4. _____
5. _____
6. _____
7. _____
8. _____
9. _____
10. _____

Us decentering men on Hannah's wedding day.

INTERLUDE:

GUYS YOU SHOULD NEVER DATE

I'M SURE THE PARENTS who graced their sons with these names had the best intentions, but something went terribly wrong. These sons had no chance of bringing peace to the world from the minute they popped out of the womb. Avoid these men at all costs, and if you ignore us and they hurt you, maybe it's a canon event, but don't say we didn't warn you.

BRAXTON: He tells his mom to shut up, and he always has chlamydia but no symptoms. He is obsessed with his Snapchat streaks and got kicked out of his high school but his parents paid hush money so no one knows what he did. He has an insanely oversize television and leather furniture that smells like Bud Light.

MATT: This below-average-looking man seems innocent, but once you fall for him, he will break your heart into shreds because you really thought there was no way this toad could disappoint you—but he will.

CHAD: This man will mansplain investment banking to you on your first date, but you won't care because you don't know anything about investing. Days later you will find out that he wears a fake Rolex and just invested all his dad's money and lost it.

BRYCE: His whole personality is that he has an ear piercing and references bands you've never heard of. He goes thrift shopping and judges you for drinking Starbucks even though he vapes every second of the day.

TANNER/TUCKER/CARTER: These are the same person. They wear Patagonia and reference their "yacht club." They secretly still think women should be homemakers and will spend more time organizing with their fantasy football draft than any date. They are also fiscally conservative.

RIVER: His dad was the producer of a famous band in the eighties and he wants you to know, but he will freak out if you bring it up. He hangs out at Soho House and travels to St. Barts, Mykonos, and Miami for Art Basel every year. He has a tattoo to remind him to breathe.

RED FLAGS IN FRIENDSHIPS

10

IF FRIENDS DISAPPOINT YOU OVER AND OVER, THAT'S IN LARGE PART YOUR OWN FAULT.

—Oprah Winfrey

RELATIONSHIPS COME IN ALL SHAPES AND FORMS. There are situationships, besties, third wheels, acquaintances, social climbers, soul mates, Instagram followers, twin flames, friends with benefits, and the list goes on. Regardless of who/what they are, they can be anxiety-inducing because they all involve social interaction. In your twenties, it's natural to want to fit in with as many people as possible, and then in your thirties it becomes all about "boundaries" and "protecting your space" and canceling plans because it's "too windy." Relationships of all kinds are mirrors to help you learn about yourself—and as a result, these interactions teach you about the kind of people you want in your circle. Friend drama and heartbreaks are all essential parts of developing a great sense of humor, so lean in and feel your feelings! Based on mistakes we've made, we've come up with friendship red flags to help you navigate the people in your life so that eventually you will be surrounded by only comfort people.

Making friends is not straightforward, and you will have a lot of different friends throughout your life. Sometimes you will feel like you have too many friends, and sometimes you will feel like you have no friends. In our experience, quality over quantity is important. You'd rather have one friend you can count on than twenty who just comment "She ate" on your Instagram pictures. You may feel like if you don't have a lot of friends, you're not doing well in life, but that's not the case. There are different types of friends for different times in your life, and recognizing what type of friendship you have with each person can help with navigating the complicated friend game.

THE FRIENDS WHO JUST WANT TO PARTY

If you love to go out and party every night, then you should. Dance, drink, make out with DJs, and puke in your purse in Ubers. As women, we always love having a wingwoman with us, and sometimes a big group of friends that are always down to party. But you should also remember that your party friends might not be the most reliable when the morning comes around. You may like each other because you both enjoy molly or weed or whatever you're into but not actually have the same friendship values. These people are great to dance with, take Insta stories with to pretend you are having the best time at the club even though you're sweaty and bloated, and text about your hangover the next day. However, these large party groups have the highest hit rate for drama. There can be weird hookups, jealousy, and gossip behind each other's backs. Whenever there are more than two friends and alcohol, it might as well be a reality TV show. Know that it is normal to fall out with some of these groups throughout your twenties. Enjoy the times you have with them and get out when the toxic levels override the fun levels. Sometimes people get scared to get out of their big friend groups because you feel like you are going from tons of friends to no friends. There is a lot of groupthink in a friend group that makes you feel weird to have your own opinion or stand up to someone who is treating everyone like shit. Sometimes people would rather be in a big friend group and be treated badly than be alone. News flash, you can feel lonelier in a huge group of friends who suck than in a small group of two cool friends who get you. Stop counting your friends, this isn't Facebook circa 2011.

THE FRIEND WHO IS ONLY
THERE WHEN YOU'RE CRYING

Some friends might be there for you in your darkest times, but then there are the friends who may be enjoying your downfall. If this type of friend asks questions or seems interested only when things are going badly, they are low-key haters or, as they say in Los Angeles, low-vibrational individuals. They love to be negative, and they love to see you when you're not doing well. They are either feeding into whatever bad drama you're going through or being cynical about other people. They are energy vampires who don't actually want to help you out of a bad place but are instead enjoying that you are feeling as bad about yourself as they are. You start to wonder if they are rooting for you to fail. Obviously it's nice to talk to someone when you're feeling down but keep an eye out for the people who only start sniffing around when something bad happens. Get out! If you surround yourself with optimistic people who have positive conversations, you will find yourself living a lighter life. The conversations you have with your friends shape your reality, and you don't want your reality to feel like a wet rag.

THE STRICTLY
MAIN-CHARACTER FRIEND

Look, we are all main characters in our own lives, but there are moments where we need to be the funny sidekick. The best part about friendships is arguably forgetting about your stupid life and getting to live vicariously through your friends. But being around a friend who only talks about themselves, or worse, turns anything you say about yourself back to them, is exhausting. They think everything revolves around them, and if it doesn't, they can cause drama to get attention. This friend is dangerous because they really don't care about you, your boundaries, or your feelings. This is the kind of person who will post a group photo where she Facetunes herself and everyone else looks like shit.

THE LEECHY FRIEND

This friend is fun in the beginning because they will love-bomb you. They are charming and make you feel like you are the only girl in the room. They will yell in your face that they "love you" the first night you meet them and then blow you up with text messages like they've known you their whole life. This could be a twin-flame moment but this could also be someone who really, really, really wants a close friend, and that is not necessarily you. They want you to text back immediately and be down to hang at any time. They also can get weird if you can't hang out or choose to spend time with other friends. They can make you feel guilty when you're like, wait, I never decided to be in a fully committed girl marriage with you! Honestly, this kind of friend gives us hives. This friend will get mad when you meet a guy and it's like, *Please stop blowing up my phone unless you're planning on going down on me.*

THE FRIEND WHO HATES GIRLIES

If you meet someone who doesn't like hanging out with girls because they "are too much drama," it's giving *All my exes are crazy*. These friends are not necessarily bad people, but they definitely have had a lot of issues with other women, and it is a pattern where they are the common denominator, and that's girl math. It's obviously easy to be "friends" with guys. Sometimes they're surrounded by guy friends because they are prioritizing men too much and that has caused issues with other friends. Once they understand that supporting women in the arts and STEM will only enhance their overall life experience with glitter and rainbows, they have the potential to be a great friend. This girlie may have been burned by a past friend, be super competitive, or have mommy issues. We don't know, and we don't care, but it's not your job to fix her, and don't take it personally if she never has your back.

THE FRIEND WHO YOU ALWAYS BOMB WITH

If a friend doesn't laugh at your jokes, they hate you. We all know that person who you can bring your top-tier bits to and they still will not even give you a giggle. This can make you feel like you are the problem and you need to do better. You think you need to be more clever, witty, and funny to get them to like you. They act like they know things you don't know and don't even acknowledge that you are a top-tier personality hire in any Forbes 500 company. You are hilarious, so they are dealing with their own issues. This person is a hater, and you really want to be around people who love your humor. If they don't think you're funny, then what are we doing? Having boring small talk with each other for the rest of our lives? Check, please, get out of there.

FRIENDSHIP HIERARCHY

1. Mom, if you have a healthy relationship

2. Best friend

3. Best friend at work

4. A couple friends who you always send memes to about your declining mental health

5. Your hometown friends who know your origin story

6. Any gay guy who gives you attention

7. Person on social media who is the first to comment on all your photos

8. The barista who knows your coffee order

9. The coworker who you see in the bathroom all the time because you have the same pooping routine after drinking your coffee

10. Your neighbor's dog who you pet sometimes

GREEN

FLAGS

IN

FRIENDSHIPS

11

HANNAH BERNER   PAIGE DESORBO

We hope you enjoy the book!

When you've finished reading, be sure to rate and review on Goodreads and anywhere else you share your thoughts on books.

We also love to see your reviews on social media. Share your posts and tag the authors **@hannahberner** and **@paige_desorbo** on Instagram, Facebook, and TikTok, and tag us **@_simonelement** on Instagram.

Happy Reading!
The Team at Simon Element

SIMON
ELEMENT

Welcome to the Elemental Readers campaign for:

HOW TO GIGGLE

by Paige Desorbo and Hannah Berner

'TIS THE PRIVILEGE OF FRIENDSHIP TO TALK NONSENSE AND TO HAVE HER NONSENSE RESPECTED.

—Charles Lamb

SENDING VOICE NOTES: If your friend doesn't take you on a full word-salad journey with long pauses and loud coughs, I don't want it. I want drama. I want tangents. I want her to remember something else mid-sentences so I get two stories for the price of one. Calling is too personal and a jump scare, so voice notes is an easy way to achieve a high level of intimacy and a creative way to tell your gossip. It's also one step away from starting a podcast.

SENDS YOU TOO MANY DMS: Spamming your friend with inside jokes, things to buy, random coffee shops in Paris you want to go to, et cetera, is an extremely important form of communication. You should feel zero shame sending hundreds of messages, even if they never respond.

OPPOSITE TASTE IN MEN: It goes without saying, but because this is a book and we have a word minimum to hit, even if it "goes without saying," I am still going to say it. It goes without saying that girl code runs deep and I would rather pull my hair out than compete for a man. There is power in having the exact opposite taste in men than your friend. It makes scanning the room for guys that much easier because you've basically clocked every man in half the time. That is women in STEM. Also, when your friend is not blindly attracted to a man, she can see the red flags that are smacking you in the face but you are ignoring.

GOING RADIO SILENT: Of course we are always there for our friends, but having a true level of understanding with your best friend is knowing when they just need a minute. Being telepathic with your bestie should not be taken lightly. Just because you don't speak for forty-eight hours doesn't mean you're in a fight. It means you discovered a new cult documentary series and you are overstimulated with your new obsession.

DOESN'T ACKNOWLEDGE HOLIDAYS: If you text your friend "Happy Thanksgiving," that is so fucking weird. It feels like you are going to ask her to join your Tupperware multilevel marketing scheme. Nobody wants your lame holiday text with a turkey emoji. Also, everyone knows random holiday texts are for your exes when they try to get back into your life but you're too busy eating dry turkey meat and fighting with your family.

DOESN'T VENMO YOU FOR COFFEE: If your "friend" Venmos you $6.47 for a matcha latte, you will immediately see them in small-claims court. It's volatile, disrespectful, and a personal attack. If they don't think they will ever see you again and don't think you're worth a Venti iced caramel macchiato with almond milk and an extra shot of espresso, then they can go fuck themselves. We wish them bad coffee breath for life.

KNOWS WHEN YOU DON'T NEED ANOTHER SHOT: True friends know when you get that certain glaze over your eyes and it's time for a water before things get out of hand. Other friends will not notice that you are about to black out and try to steal a taxi, but your good friends will protect you from having to go to jail, or worse, texting your ex.

HAS A DIFFERENT GOOD SIDE IN PHOTOS: After you spend three hours getting ready while listening to "Espresso" for the four hundred millionth time, it is finally time to get "the photo." Your makeup, hair, and outfits are eating, but when it's time to find the right post, you cannot be fighting over who stands on which side. If you both have the same side, one of you will have to distort their neck like an owl or you will have to commit to a weird prom pose so that you both look good. Luckily, Paige doesn't have a bad side because she's a Limited Too model, so she lets Hannah pick her own good side. In every photo, Hannah will strategically be on the left because the right side of her face looks like a mole rat.

MAKES A FINSTA TO STALK YOUR ENEMIES: It's obviously not emotionally healthy to stalk people in your life who you hate, but if you're going to do it, have your best friend do it for you. They will tell you all the tea you need to know and also protect you from information that doesn't serve you. They will move in silence and not bring any suspicion toward you. Let's just say the second your ex starts balding, your best friend will let you know.

TELLS YOU WHEN YOUR OUTFIT IS UGLY: Your best friend wants the best for you and will always be honest with you. She is not hurting your feelings but rather helping you always look your best. She takes the time to look through all your clothes to pick the perfect outfit because you are an extension of her. You may have completely opposite styles, like Hannah and Paige, but you respect each other's brand and what makes each other feel confident. Paige's favorite thing to say when Hannah puts on a hunting T-shirt with Adidas pants is "That outfit is very you."

HOW TO BE IN BUSINESS WITH YOUR BEST FRIEND

A LOT OF PEOPLE WILL TELL YOU not to go into business with your best friend. Someone even said, "Don't shit where you eat," which is gross and unnecessary but can be true. Just because you have compatibility as friends doesn't mean you can run a company together. It's almost like when you get along with someone but then you ask them to be your roommate and you realize that they hoard glasses in their room and take fifty-minute showers and have a smelly boyfriend who visits too often and you actually can't stand them. It's definitely important to truly know someone before jumping into business with them. We never planned to start a business together but slowly gained trust in each other. First we survived filming reality TV together, which is a high-stress situation where you can form alliances or enemies. We immediately were looking out for each other and were honest with each other when things were getting spicy. If we heard someone was planning to start drama or ask a difficult question, we would go into the bathroom and put our hands on our mics or text each other. We wanted each other to be successful on the show, and with every difficult moment that we survived, our friendship got stronger. Every time we could have fallen apart, instead we chose each other and got closer.

We realized that there were also parts of our personalities that made us good at working together, whether we are riffing on a joke or deciding what the title of this book should be. A lot of people want to have business partners who think similarly to them, but we have benefitted from being very different. For example, Hannah hates getting glam. She hates picking outfits and worrying about how everything is going to look. Turns out, Paige lives for getting glam and holds Hannah's hand and makes sure that at every show they both feel confident and beautiful before they perform. Meanwhile, Hannah loves coming up with business ideas and being creative. Paige is really good at being decisive and picking which ideas are great and which should be tarred and feathered.

We do have a lot of similarities that make us compatible in running a business though. We both have the same communication style. We are very honest with each other, and it takes a lot for us to get annoyed with each other. We are pretty laid-back and understand that we are both out here trying our best. If Paige doesn't text Hannah back, it's because she's napping, and vice versa. We also both really believe in each other, so when one of us is questioning herself or feeling down, the other reminds her that she is the greatest (but with no hugging because we have intimacy issues). Behind every great girl is a great friend. That was corny, but we are sticking to it.

Going on tour took our friendship to the next level. We were dealing with new logistics and pressure. Paige wanted an Uber XL, but Hannah got a Camry. Paige wanted Hannah to do a slicked-back bun, but Hannah thought she looked like a hard-boiled egg. Paige wasn't sure she was ready to perform multiple shows a night, but Hannah knew that Paige would chug an espresso martini and nail it. Thankfully, we both love sleeping in, resting our voices, meeting Gigglers, gossiping during any downtime, and ordering Uber Eats so it arrives at the hotel exactly when we get back from the show.

We are not telling you to quit your job and start a business with your best friend immediately, but keep an eye out for people who you jive with (do people say that?) and who are authentically rooting for you. Sometimes you are stronger with a partner who tells you when your outfit is disgusting and it's time to throw away your smelly fur Crocs and brush your hair.

When the beta-blocker hits.

RED FLAGS IN ROMANTIC RELATIONSHIPS

12

SOME THINGS BREAK YOUR HEART BUT FIX YOUR VISION.

—Steve Maraboli

NOW THAT YOU'VE CUT OFF ALL YOUR FRIENDS, let's discuss romantic relationships. No matter how good you are at decentering men from your life, you still will occasionally bump into them. If that happens, take a deep breath, take off your rose-colored glasses, and try to see their red flags. We are positive and optimistic angels, so when we meet a new man, we assume he's perfect and then wait for him to show us he's not. This makes it difficult to see red flags because you are rooting for him and making excuses for him! Try this instead: When you first meet a guy, assume he's trash and let him prove to you that he's not. Guys are tricky though, especially if they are tall, have a scruffy beard, had a hot ex-girlfriend, have a trust fund, or are very average so they make you think they could never hurt you. Their name is usually Matt, and—news flash—he will. Here are some red flags to look out for, and listen to "Thank U, Next" in the background if you want to get pumped up.

THE SELF-PROCLAIMED GOOD GUY

This man is a monster. If he tells you on the first date that he's a "good guy," that means he has bodies in his basement. That's like if you have to tell people that you're funny, then you're not fucking funny. That's like if you have to tell people that you're not drunk. You're fucking blackout. The fact that he is saying that he is a good guy means he is being defensive because multiple people have told him that he's not a good guy, or, even worse, he knows he's not a good guy. Guys will lie to your face to try to make you like them, and it's embarrassing for everyone in the room. Also, what the hell does it even mean to be a "good guy"? Like you don't cheat? You call your mom once a week? You send money to save the elephants every month? Ask him what he legitimately means by that because we would love to know. All I hear is that this guy has ruined lives and you don't want to be his next victim.

THE GUY WHO IS TOO ACTIVE ON SOCIAL MEDIA

This is by far the scariest man on the list. If he takes selfies, mirror pics, or photos with his friends, he is unwell. How do straight men even take photos together? They stop the conversation and find a stranger to capture a photo of the moment? Ick central. If he cares about his social presence, he is a twisted motherfucker. Also, if he posts multiple Insta stories a day, see you in court. Men cannot be president, start wars, always orgasm during sex, and have a stellar social media presence. It's giving dehydrated.

THE GUY WHO TELLS YOU HE LIKES YOU IMMEDIATELY

This man doesn't know you. If a man tells you that he has feelings on a first date, he is just telling you what you want to hear so he can try to finger you awkwardly and then ask if you came. Saying that you like someone is a way to make that person trust you. Don't trust him until he shows you that he is worthy of being trusted. Also, remember to keep your head in the game. Once a guy says he likes you, it's easy to miss the red flags because you are flattered and think he has amazing taste. You have to focus on whether YOU LIKE HIM. If a guy earnestly says he likes you on the first date, he seems like a snake-oil salesman, and for that I'm out.

THE GUY WHOSE FRIENDS SUCK

Have you ever met a guy who seems great and then you meet his friends and they are all misogynistic assholes? Then when you ask him why his friends are so immature, he says that he hates that they are like that. He's lying. As the English proverb says, birds of a feather flock together. Men are simple creatures who hang out with people who like the same stuff as them. They don't talk about anything important, and they are so bad at gossip, the only thing they have is similar hobbies. So if all his friends are cheaters who don't respect women, get out of there and never text that pigeon back.

THE GUY WHO FOLLOWS
INSTAGRAM MODELS

Look, if he follows some Instagram models over the years, that's fine. We are talking about men who follow hundreds of Instagram models, or worse, comments fire emojis on their pages. Do not get jealous if you see a guy following tons of Instagram models. Get turned off. It's weird. If he wants to look at soft-core porn, he can do that on his own time. The fact that he does it publicly is weird and thirsty and he probably posts selfies and is obsessed with going to Mykonos with his boys.

THE GUY WHO CALLED YOU A FEMALE

This man talks about women like they are foreign objects or specimens that he doesn't understand. He believes in traditional gender roles and complains about gold diggers even though he still lives with his mom. He is still upset about getting rejected by his crush in second grade, and as a result, he hates women. He's obsessed with being considered "alpha" because his dad is disappointed in him and he has an ugly penis. He also has never made a woman orgasm and thinks the clit is a myth. I feel like you guys get the point.

THE GUY WHO HIDES HIS FEELINGS

As the psychic said to Kyle Richards on *The Real Housewives of Beverly Hills*, this man will never emotionally fulfill you. At first he's fun because he's mysterious and never serious and you don't know what he's thinking. But eventually it gets old because he has the emotional maturity of a guinea pig and whenever you want to talk about anything remotely serious he will make you feel like you're talking to a brick wall. He thinks therapy is "stupid" and nothing has ever been his fault. This man doesn't understand himself, so there is no way he will ever understand you.

THE GUY WHO TALKS ABOUT HIS EXES

This man is trying to remind you that other people have liked him before and he could not be more lame for this. Whether he compares you to them or just name-drops them, he is trying to make you jealous. We love a little natural jealousy because it's flirty, hot, and shows you care, but him actively trying to piss you off is grounds for kicking his ass out. If he is just bashing his exes all the time, that's also a red flag because that's how he's going to talk about you. Also, they did not all trick him into dating them. He either has horrible taste or he is the problem and you don't want to be involved with either.

THE GUY WHO NEEDS A BABYSITTER

We do not have the time to raise our boyfriend. I don't care how much of a caretaker you are, it is not your job to take care of his entire life. Even if it feels nice at first to cook for him or clean up after him or do his laundry, eventually you are going to resent him. We don't have time to live our own lives and also be entirely responsible for his life. He is a grown-up and not your child. If you ever have a family with this man, you will be the only adult in the household, and that is above our paygrade. Just think of the admin! A man that can't take care of himself is so not cute. If there is a zombie apocalypse, he would die immediately, and that is such a turnoff.

*When it comes to our lesbian Gigglers, we do not have enough research on our end to speak from a place of authority for your red flags, but you will probably miss them because you are having so many multiple orgasms. When the battery dies or you get carpal tunnel, try to see her for who she really is, but this is easier said than done. Because of this conundrum, we don't judge you for moving in with her immediately.

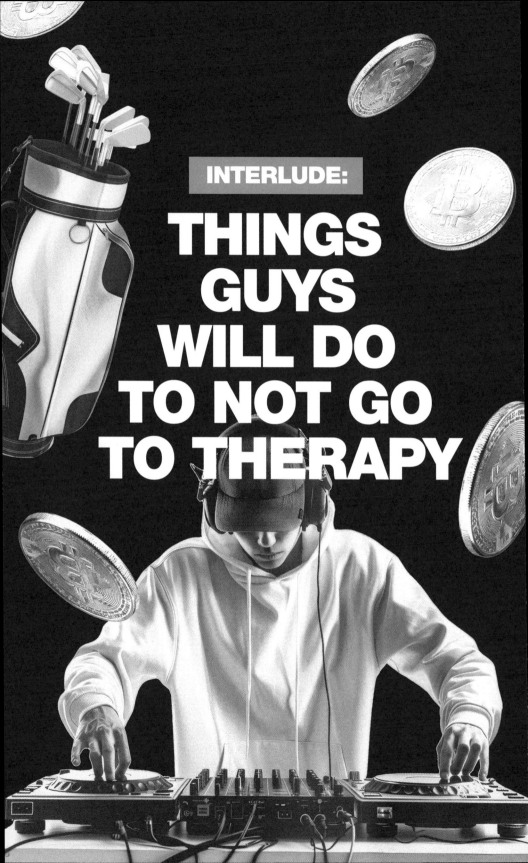

INTERLUDE:

THINGS GUYS WILL DO TO NOT GO TO THERAPY

- START WAR

- NO-SHAVE NOVEMBER

- LEARN MANDARIN

- "GOLF TRIPS"

- HAVE SECOND FAMILIES

- PARKOUR

- "PLAY" THE GUITAR

- START A PILLOW COMPANY

- AX THROWING

- GASLIGHTING

- GET A HAIRCUT

- NOT USE CONDOMS

- RUN FOR PRESIDENT

- BUY BITCOIN

- GET A CALF TATTOO

- SAY THEY CAN'T BELIEVE YOU HAVEN'T SEEN (INSERT MOB MOVIE)

- START A PODCAST

- BECOME A "SNEAKERHEAD"

- CROSSFIT

- GET A DRAFTKINGS ACCOUNT

- BECOME A DJ

- JOIN A SPORTS TEAM AFTER COLLEGE

- PUNCH WALLS

GREEN FLAGS IN ROMANTIC RELATIONSHIPS

13

We can't think of any.

HOW TO POOP IN PUBLIC

WHEN YOU LEAVE THE COMFORT OF YOUR HOME, you will inevitably find yourself in a precarious situation if you need to poop. Most of society pretends women don't poop, so we have to pretend that all the Taco Bell we just ate evaporates into Santal 33 eau de parfum as it slowly gets released through our pores as we sweat. Unfortunately, that is not the case for anyone and we have both shat ourselves in public. Pooping your pants is actually more common than you think, and it happens to some of the greatest minds. Here are some of our tips for navigating your bowel movements in public.

AT WORK

Pooping at work is truly an art form. When we had nine-to-fives our days were just sitting in the bathroom with a couple meetings in between. Similar to a party (damn open-plan offices) you don't want to make it obvious how many times you are going to the bathroom, so you need to be around different colleagues each time you make a beeline to the bathroom. Also, try going at random times so you don't get stuck in the same bathroom pattern as someone else. Small talk with the same coworker every time you are in the bathroom will ruin this very cathartic experience. If you are going to finally leave your desk, you don't want to have added stress. Being in the work bathroom alone is ideal or, if you can't swing that, going with a friend who doesn't care that you are about to spend ten minutes in the bathroom shitting and crying. If you've never done this, you are not a woman of the arts. Try it. You're welcome.

AT A BAR

Whenever you get to a place you're going to be at for a while, immediately clock where the bathroom is. This way, you can quietly go whenever you need to without making a scene. If you're feeling gassy, just make sure there are men around you because no one will ever assume that a dainty flower like yourself is capable of ripping such a disgustingly hot fart. The guys will blame each other, and you can just play dumb. If you have to poop, bathrooms at these establishments are normally huge, and everyone's drunk, so no one cares. Let that shit go! You can even joke with your girlfriend about having to drop the kids off at the pool and she will laugh and you will hit a new level of friendship. If it's really loud, just flush during it. Whatever you do, don't hold it in. Life is too short, and you want to comfortably go have uncomfortable conversations with strangers at the bar!

ON A DATE

We highly recommend going to the bathroom during a date. Let him reflect on how amazing you are and take a second to stop pretending you're perfect in the quiet of a bathroom stall. The problem is that there are a lot of social norms that come with going to the bathroom on a date, and you have to do it correctly. Firstly, you can only go to the bathroom once during the date or he might assume you have bladder problems or food poisoning. Secondly, if you are planning on going to his place after the date you should definitely go to the bathroom at dinner so you are less likely to take a shit at his place. Knowing this, make sure you don't go to the bathroom too early in the date because then you've used your only bathroom break. Focus, girlies! It's literally a match at Wimbledon! Finally, if you happen to be in the bathroom for a while, maybe you're a little constipated or dealing with a period with a heavy flow, when you get back to the table you can lie and say, "Sorry, there was a line." You also have the option of ignoring all these rules and going to the bathroom five times during the date and when you get back say, "Wow, I feel ten pounds lighter." If he is your soul mate, he will find this endearing or even hot.

AT HIS APARTMENT

Okay, this is the most difficult of them all. This can make or break relationships early on. When the universe is mad at you, sometimes you will have to poop at his place. Some women in STEM will bring around matches so after they go, they light the match and it helps with the smell. Some women will just turn on the faucet and pray. Some women will flush multiple times so it doesn't have time to smell up the room. But if it's a real problem, some women will literally go to "pick up tampons" or when he's asleep sneak out and go to the nearest bar, Starbucks, coffee shop, or Barnes & Noble, if they still exist. You can also wake up early in the morning to grab breakfast, which is code for, get out your morning shit in a safe place. If all of this seems too overwhelming to you, tell him that you have to poop, and if he acts weird, then take his phone, Venmo yourself $300, and leave. There is a wage gap, and we are fixing it one bad date on Hinge at a time.

AWKWARD

MOMENTS

IN

BED

14

IF YOU DON'T LAUGH DURING SEX AT LEAST ONCE, YOU'RE HAVING SEX WITH THE WRONG PERSON.

—Anonymous

THE MEDIA LIKES TO PRETEND THAT SEX is always this hot and steamy, eyes-rolling-in-the-back-of-your-head experience. We are here to confirm that it is not. Sex can sometimes be good, but it can also be weird, awkward, and embarrassing. Once you can accept that it's okay that things aren't always perfect in bed, you can actually relax a little and maybe even have an orgasm, if you're lucky! Let's normalize that sex isn't perfect, even though we are. It's our duty to give you our honest opinion of sex because society is lying to you!

KISSING: How can the most simple, straightforward foreplay have so many things that can go wrong? Everyone is paranoid about their breath. Whether you're a little dehydrated because you haven't drank water since 1998 or you accidentally ate raw onions in guacamole a week ago, bad breath can ruin a relationship! It's a lot of pressure, and it's almost impossible to smell your own breath. Walking around with Listerine and floss and a toothbrush is too much admin, so sometimes you just have to pray. Then, your lips cannot be chapped or it's like making out with a crocodile, but they also can't be too wet or it's like eating an oyster. After stressing about all that, you still haven't even executed the actual kiss! As your lips touch, an avalanche of problems begins to flood your mind. Are you following his lead? Why are we changing the rhythm every five seconds? What weird dance with our tongues is this? Or worse, you can't find his tongue, like does he even have a tongue? Or he starts poking you too hard with his tongue like a turtle? It's hard out here in these streets.

HAND JOBS: Look, hand jobs are great when you are in high school and you don't want to have sex, but once you become an adult, he can give himself a hand job. We are never going to do it as well as he can and after a couple pumps your hand gets sore. Some guys like it fast, slow, hard, loose, dry, wet, and it's too many options. If you are comfortable, just put your mouth on it, that is the best move.

BLOW JOBS: We always wonder, who was the first human who thought, *I want to put that thing that he pees with in my mouth?* The hardest part about blow jobs is becoming an Oscar-winning actress and pretending that it's the most fun thing you've done all day and all you want to do is get gagged by his meat stick. There is always that moment when you think you might actually puke, especially when you've had seven tequila sodas. Many of us have puked on his dick before because we are women in the arts.

CHOKING: Paige famously likes choking, and Hannah would prefer to live. There is a certain technique to it that people mess up. Sometimes they choke too hard and you get scared, but sometimes it's too soft and you're like, are you a little bitch? There are many things that can go wrong. It can be hard to orgasm while also fighting for your life, but we would never yuck someone's yum. Choking involves a healthy amount of consent, trust, and daddy issues to work properly.

CUNNILINGUS: I feel like some women can either only come when a guy is going down on her or she literally hates it. We are either coming in five minutes or five to seven business days, and no one talks about this phenomenon. It is vulnerable to let a guy eat your pink taco and know that if he looks up he will see the exact angle that you see when you accidentally open your phone on selfie mode. Who knew you could have so many chins? The worst is if he prides himself for being a "giver" but then just does the ABCs, and whenever it starts to accidentally feel good, he always changes the rhythm. There is also the slim chance that while you're trying really hard to orgasm in spite of his terrible technique, you can accidentally push out a fart. Hannah famously did this to her ex "British Dave," who couldn't get a boner for months after the incident.

SITTING ON HIS FACE: This is arguably harder than riding him. No one tells you that you don't actually sit on his face, you have to squat and hover like you're at a port-a-potty at Coachella. Your thighs will start to burn, and if he's a hockey player, so will your pussy. You never know what to do with your hands because it feels weird to pat his forehead while he's staring up at you like he's getting waterboarded. Guys already have trouble with regular cunnilingus, so don't expect him to suddenly be good at reverse cunnilingus.

SEX IN THE BATHROOM: There are many things that can go wrong with sex in the bathroom. You can be looking at the mirror and making weird eye contact with each other and you don't know if you should look away but then you notice that you have a pimple and you don't love how your arm looks and you also want to move your hair. If you try to do it in the shower, this can also be a nightmare. Men and women like different water temperatures. Women like it scorching hot because we are related to Satan, and men like it lukewarm because they are confused. And, if you're in his shower, he won't have hair conditioner but he will have the three-in-one, which is the devil's ejaculate. You also have to find time to put your hair on his shower wall and in his butt crack in order to mark your territory. This is a lot of admin. Finally, remember that water is not lube and somehow it makes everything more dry. We are not women in STEM, so we don't know the science behind it but it will not feel good. Period.

Also for the record, Hannah and Des never had sex in that bathroom. They were told to act like they were fooling around in a bunch of different rooms in the house, and then they just showed one bathroom with added noises. See you in the supreme court.

DOGGY: We like when a guy is behind us during sex because it means we can text without him knowing. However, when you turn around, he can get confused and "accidentally" hit the wrong hole. Thankfully, our buttholes have the reflexes of a ninja and will always block him immediately. Sometimes if there is a dog in the room, you can feel like they are judging your technique. This position always makes a very loud smacking sound, and it might be his ball sack hitting your leg or his head hitting your hymen, we have no clue.

RIDING HIM: We are exhausted even writing this. Some women can only orgasm in this position, and then some women would rather lie on their back and do nothing. We support them both. There are different techniques, some people like to go up and down and others like to go back and forth. This variation of technique leaves a lot of room for error. Getting into the same rhythm can be difficult. If his dick accidentally slips out, you can snap it like a glowstick. Drama.

BDSM: That is a perfect segue to talk about the slapstick of sex. It involves a lot of accessories and boxes and knowing how to tie things, which seems like a lot of admin. Also we live in NYC, so if we decided that we liked BDSM, we would have to figure out how to fit a dungeon in our small apartments. Paige would never replace her closet for a Pilates reformer sex studio, but she once almost broke up with a boyfriend after watching an Italian man named Massimo tie up a woman in the movie *365 Days* on Netflix, but we digress.

69: Just don't.

INTERLUDE:

NICHE ICKS

THESE SPECIFIC ICKS MIGHT CHANGE YOUR BRAIN CHEMISTRY, SO WE APOLOGIZE IN ADVANCE.

- When he gets the hiccups and can't get rid of them.

- When he chases the beer pong ball.

- When he's angry in flip-flops.

- When he holds his nose in water.

- When he sits crisscross applesauce.

- When he texts with this emoji 😄

- When he says he has a side hustle.

- When he taste-tests ice cream with the baby spoon.

- When he bowls and his leg goes up behind him.

- When he breathes.

HOW TO

FLIRT

15

WHAT YOU SEEK IS SEEKING YOU.
—Rūmī

OUR ONLY HOBBY IN THIS WORLD IS FLIRTING. We don't collect stamps, we don't basketweave, and we actually can't even think of any other possible hobbies. We flirt. It's an art form, and there is strategy, and we will walk you through our process. Flirting is a great skill to have because you can feel confident when making the first move because sometimes the person you think is attractive is shy, terrified, and scared. Also, most important, flirting is fun and silly and so not serious. Putting yourself out there can be intimidating, but once you get the hang of it, it's easy. Why wait for someone to choose you?

The first key to flirting is getting your mindset right. You are not putting yourself out there to be rejected, you are just having fun talking to hot people and feeling the vibes. It's like doing crowd work onstage, what's the worst that can happen? The conversation goes badly? Then you say "Good chat" or "Am I awkward?" or "I'm going to get a drink!" The stakes are very low. Also, you should only care what your best friends think of you. They matter, and they care. Who cares about a weird conversation with drunk people at the bar? Also, if the conversation is meant to go well, it will. People don't remember what you said, they remember how you made them feel. If your energies match up, it will flow, and if it doesn't, the universe did not want you with them anyway.

Okay, now that your head is in the game, let's talk strategy. You don't need to work up the confidence to approach someone to give them a compliment. It doesn't have to feel forced or awkward. Here are some moves.

THE LONG GAME

This is a fun way to trick someone into talking to you. You can also see if they are into you without having to put yourself out there. The key is to start talking to someone in their friend group who is less intimidating. Once you see that your crush has noticed your interaction, the game begins. You can stay in the group and talk, or you can leave and then pop back up throughout the night for some fun interactions. If your crush is into you, you are giving them the opening to say something to you while you are now cool with their buddies. If they don't say anything to you, maybe they aren't into it, and that's fine. You didn't get rejected. Also, worst-case scenario, you made some friends. If you think they didn't say anything because they are intimidated by how beautiful and confident you are as you run the room, you can throw a little attention their way. This works 90 percent of the time and is not awkward whatsoever.

THE SACRIFICIAL FRIEND

We are huge fans of this trend because it involves having a wing-woman. Paige is a little more shy than Hannah, so whenever she spots someone cute at the bar (when she was single!), she sends Hannah to start a conversation. Hannah has no pressure to be smooth or cool. She can be silly, funny, and even weird, as per usual. Paige will then come to the rescue, and Hannah will introduce her to the guy. You're basically buttering them up for your other friend to save the day.

THE POKE

This one takes a little bit of charisma or "rizz," as the kids are saying. If you notice something about him that you can make a sarcastic comment about, go for it. Sometimes people will be too mean when they try to flirt, and it goes terribly wrong. Take it easy. Some good examples are if you see a muscular guy, ask him, "Do you work out?" Or if he is wearing a bright shirt, say, "I wish your shirt was brighter." The key is to not try too hard with the comment, you are basically opening the conversation with some humor. If you try too hard to be too funny, it can come off corny. Do not take this too seriously! At the end of the day, if they think you're cute, you can fart on their leg and they will like it.

THE ACCIDENT

This is for anyone who is reading this like, *Are you fucking kidding me? I'm way too shy for any of these moves*. Well, good news for you, we have some tricks that don't involve any skill. First, just stand near them. At the bar, in a line, dancing, just put yourself in their ether. You can also accidentally bump into them (not too hard, don't be a linebacker) and then smile. A smile goes a long way. If you're feeling a little gutsy, you can ask them a question like, "Has this been taking a long time?" or "Is someone in the bathroom?" or "Is that drink good?" Finally, you can *Legally Blonde* it and pull a bend and snap by dropping your purse near his foot. This can be dangerous though, if he's a robber.

SMIZING

This is for my ultra-shy girlies—the black cats of the group. Showing just enough attention but then immediately withdrawing. If you were on *America's Next Top Model,* your instructions would be to look your crush up and down quickly once. When he's talking, stare at his lips for a few seconds, then his eyes. Adding in a little smirk while balancing being uninterested. Now this is trial and error of course, as my orbital bone is not aligned with our mission figuratively and literally, and you may look like a wounded animal, but it builds character.

THE SILENT TREATMENT

Don't do anything and pray to St. Anthony. If he doesn't come over to talk to you, that was not your journey and you had a great time with your friend.

MOM MATH

16

IT'S NOT EASY BEING A MOM. IF IT WERE EASY, FATHERS WOULD DO IT.

—Betty White

AN EXCERPT FROM HANNAH'S MOM, LENORE

HI, GIGGLERS! HANNAH'S MOM, Lenore, here! Like many moms, it's hard for us not to add our two cents to things that involve our children. So when Hannah asked me to review the book and give feedback, I immediately put on my teacher hat and corrected grammar and sentence structure (with Paige's permission, I did the same for her, LOL). So if paragraphs make a little more sense, sentences are less awkward, or you're impressed by their vocabulary, that's my fault. Why ask your mom to do this when you have the best publishers in the business? Well, because, mom math.

No one knows a millennial better than their own mom. Moms' brains use very special, maternal (dare I say, psychic) calculations that help their children (young or grown) function in the wild, while simultaneously tracking and assessing safety and progress. From the moment your child is born, you begin to carefully monitor their eating, sleeping, moods, skills, and hygiene—an intuitive skill that only becomes a more precise science with your age and theirs.

Is your head swirling from decision overload and politics at work? Discuss it with your mom and your brain will lean clearly toward a solution. Feeling cranky, PMS-y, or scared, just call or hug your mom. I'm not suggesting codependency, coddling, arrested development, or helicopter parenting. On the contrary, Kim and I raised two of the strongest, funniest, hardest-working women out there by being role models and supporting our daughters' dreams. We, like many moms, juggled careers, momhood, friendships, finances, and marriage, while supporting the growth of our children. If you've been a mom for any amount of time, you have developed a unique, supportive parenting mindset that we call mom math.

FOR EXAMPLE: At any time of day, you know exactly when your child is about to be hungry (or thirsty), so you carry snacks in case you're between meals. Is your child acting cranky—first question, "When have you last eaten anything?" You knew it would happen, and you're prepared. Why does Hannah always carry snack bars in her purse? It's not just because we're Italian. She learned from me to have one handy, as she was always starving before, during, and after tennis practice and couldn't wait for a meal. Anything to avoid hangry Hannah!

Now that Hannah is a grown, married adult, we no longer live together and we don't even speak every day, so mom math needs to kick into a higher gear. Although we may still text or DM a bit— and she always sends me cat videos, so I know she's alive, I get a bit concerned when too much time or even days go by without direct contact. I can obviously follow her Insta stories to know her whereabouts, but my secret is that I am the only person in the world who has her location in my Find My Friends app (hehe). I did not have this information when she was a child. Hannah had her first iPhone in college, probably around 2011, and I didn't have access to her location until she put it in my phone around 2018, as a joke. This was an incredible and valuable amount of data added to my mom math calculations! It reduced the number of texts necessary to gather information and allowed me to connect the dots to the daily mysteries of Hannah's whereabouts—whose apartment she stayed at (before Des), where she was eating her meals, and what time she got home from a night out in the big city. I'm absolutely sure that the Gigglers' amazing investigative skills come from their moms.

Even with the location finder, your child's whereabouts can be perplexing and require more complicated mom math. Whenever Hannah does not respond to calls, emails, texts, and DMs, I've learned to trust the process and not panic. SHE'S SLEEPING. Even though it's the middle of the day, she's a tired girlie and has simply fallen asleep for a few hours. This discovery has taken years of study, making me an advanced momamatician!

Unfortunately, mom math is not always positive. Sometimes we're not happy with the information we've gathered and can't sleep. One night, I said to my husband, "I'm sensing Hannah's flight is delayed and that there is a problem with her hotel." When she finally called the next day and told me of her travel horrors, all I could say was, "I know. I figured it out yesterday."

Here are more examples of negative mom math:

- When it's one hour before showtime and the data shows she still hasn't left the hotel, you know it's time to text or call because she's in deep REM and the snooze button is being pressed multiple times.

- Mom math knows the difference between a run-of-the-mill stomachache and appendicitis. So when Hannah was writhing in pain and I told her we were going to the hospital, she didn't fight me. Yes, it was appendicitis.

- Paige described Kim's mom math special power as the precise timing and asking of questions during a phone call. Kim can sense when something is off. She will chitchat a bit, then carefully ask a few key questions and wait for the tears.

- When you see a picture of her on Instagram and you can tell by the hairdo and outfit that it's time to remind her to shower and do laundry. Is that too mean?

AN EXCERPT FROM PAIGE'S MOM, KIM

PAIGE WAS BORN INTO A BIG ITALIAN FAMILY, and like many other large families, there is a proclivity for passing down traditions. One of the prevailing traditions of our family has always been to show and spread love through not only the preparation and serving of food but during the time spent around the table. That's mom math!

Growing up, Paige was nearly inseparable from my mother, her grandmother Rosemary. With her, Paige learned firsthand the thoughtfulness and care behind preparing a dish for those around your table, the time and attention to detail in picking fresh, healthy ingredients, and the satisfaction of watching a loved one truly enjoy their meal.

Many of our fondest family memories are around the table, because it is more than where we eat, it is where we share our thoughts, experiences, and instill our family values, but overall for my family it is a place to feel and share love.

Keeping that in mind, as Paige's grandmother certainly had taught her, sometimes the best recipes are the least complex and easily doubled or tripled, this way even in a pinch, the food on the table can live up to the importance of who is seated.

CHERRY TOMATO AND BASIL SAUCE

SIMPLE PASTA DISH RECIPE

INGREDIENTS
SERVES 4-6

2 tbsp. of olive oil

2 pints of cherry tomatoes (If you are fortunate enough to have a garden and pick the cherry tomatoes off vine just before you make the sauce it makes the world of difference in the flavor.)

½ tsp. crushed red pepper flakes optional (Only add if you want a little spice.)

3 cloves of garlic, chopped

salt and pepper, to taste

10–15 basil leaves (Additional leaves for garnish. For garnish, chiffonade basil leaves—roll leaves and slice.)

¼ cup of Parmesan cheese, additional to top each dish

1 lb. spaghetti (Buy pasta imported from Italy and ALWAYS cook al dente.)

1. Before you start your sauce, boil water for the spaghetti. Add salt to pasta water (about 2 tbsp.).

2. On medium heat, add olive oil to sauce pan, once oil is heated, add cherry tomatoes and salt and pepper to taste. Cover and let simmer for a few minutes, stir occasionally. Once tomatoes start blistering and releasing juices, add chopped garlic. Stir for about 60 seconds. Lower heat to low and cover.

3. Once pasta is cooked, reserve a cup of pasta water. Drain pasta and add on top of cherry tomato sauce, add basil and Parmesan cheese on top of pasta. Before you toss pasta with sauce, remove from heat. If pasta is dry, add some of reserved pasta water.

4. Once plated, add more Parmesan and top with basil garnish.

NOTE: A pasta dish should be served with Italian bread (buy the best bread that you can; if you can go to a real bakery, I highly recommend that), a salad, and a nice glass of wine.

Once you master this simple pasta sauce, it can be the base for so many other dishes. One of my favorites is adding cod and capers to the sauce.

INTERLUDE:

WHAT WE WANT TO TEACH OUR DAUGHTERS

PAIGE

WHEN I WAS YOUNGER, ORGANIZED sports just weren't for me. I thought the outfits were itchy, I didn't like getting dirty, and I wasn't good at any individualized sports. Figure skating lessons were a nightmare. When I first started modeling, I didn't get the concept of "not booking a job." I actually didn't even know I was ever auditioning for something, let alone a job. All I knew was that I went into a studio with my mom, they would ask my name, take my picture, and that was the whole thing. I was just happy I got out of school early, could eat a bagel in the car, and nap on the way home.

It wasn't until I started to get a little older and could understand the difference between the audition and the actual photoshoot. I then started to realize that different photo shoots were for different brands. I became more interested when there were toys on set that I actually got to play with. I remember this distinct audition that was for Barbie, and I really wanted to get it. I really wanted this job specifically because I wanted to see all the Barbies and their clothes.

After multiple rounds of auditions one day, I asked my mom what ever happened to the Barbie audition and if I booked it. She swiftly said, "They picked a little girl with blonde hair," and moved on. At my young age of rationalizing I thought, *Oh I don't even have blond hair so who cares.*

I learned years later that they did not, in fact, pick a blond girl and picked a girl who looked exactly like me who later went on to star in her own Disney Channel show. I asked my mom why she would make up the "they picked a blond girl" story and not tell me the truth. She said, "I told you that because you were so young and because you had brown hair, so logically they couldn't have picked you." She said it worked because I never felt rejected. She would just always tell me, "Oh, they picked a blonde," even if they hadn't. I realized at that moment my mom had taught me that it's irrelevant to compare yourself to anyone. In that one answer I feel like she instilled self-esteem—knowing you're different from everyone and that uniqueness is what makes you beautiful. One of the many things I want to teach my daughter is to not compare herself to

what anyone else is doing. Rejection truly is redirection, so if you are passed up for a promotion or your boyfriend breaks up with you for a literal blonde, it's because it wasn't meant to be and there is no point in comparing yourself because you're different and that's the best compliment.

HANNAH

This is a fun little message for our unborn daughters. I'm afraid to write this and then jinx myself and have a son named Braxton, but I can't live in fear. If I ever have a daughter, I want to emphasize to her that her worth is not in being pretty, or being agreeable, or being liked by boys. A lot of the time when we see a little girl, we immediately call her "pretty" and if we see a boy, we call him "strong," "smart," or "athletic." These words affect how kids feel about themselves, and I never want my daughter to only feel worth in her looks. I want her to find value in kindness, strength, and intelligence. I want her to play with LEGO blocks and tennis balls and Barbies. I want her to know that she can be anything she wants, but also that it's okay to not know what you want. From a young age, I want her to feel like she can be independent and solve problems on her own (or with a little help from her mom or her dad if mom is napping). I also want her to one day read this book because I want her to live a life of giggles. If Paige and I don't have funny children, we will put them up for adoption.

THINGS YOU

SHOULD

NOT

FORCE

17

IT IS BETTER TO TRAVEL WELL THAN TO ARRIVE.

—Buddha

WE LOVE TO FORCE THINGS. But it's not our fault, we are anxious about the future and want everything to work out perfectly, as it should because we are adorable! Turns out, forcing things never works. Forcing things actually causes tension, resistance, and anxiety. It can actually backfire and make things worse. Let us give you some examples.

Let's begin with something simple like pooping. If you force it, you can get hemorrhoids and die (allegedly). Relax, drink some coffee, trust the process, and it will happen when it's meant to happen. Whenever you are forcing something to happen in life, just think about bowel movements and you will be a Zen master.

Friendships are something that cannot be forced. Sometimes, when you try to force someone to like you or hang out with you, it actually makes them want to hang out with you less. If you decide not to force friendships, you will save a ton of time interacting with the wrong energies and instead see who you naturally connect with. The same goes with romantic relationships. You can work your butt off to research what a guy likes and trick him into thinking you're really into house music and that you love drinking IPAs and sleeping on his dirty navy sheets. Three months later, you have a boyfriend who you hate and you've developed cystic acne from sleeping on his pillows. People always talk about never giving up regardless of what happens, but sometimes giving up is the best thing you can do! Normalize quitting something that isn't right for you! You don't have to listen to dubstep to get dick! It's great to be proactive and go for things, but if it is too forced, sometimes that is a sign that it's not meant for you, and that's okay. If you try to control everything around you, it's super stressful and you can find yourself on the wrong path. It's scary to let things unfold, but sometimes those things are the most beautiful. The best poops ever come when you least expect them.

Many other things are better when you don't force them. Hannah's mom is a jazz singer, and when she tries too hard to hit the note, her vocal cords become tense and it doesn't sound as good. When she trusts her voice and enjoys the process of singing the song, the notes come easy and she sings her best. The same goes with tennis. When Hannah was trying to hit the ball perfectly or really hard, she would actually play worse. To play well she actually had to be relaxed and trust her instincts that she would know what to do at the right time. Paige is like this when putting together outfits. You can tell when someone is trying too hard with their outfit or questioning themselves. When in doubt, put on a Zara set and chill the fuck out. When we first started recording our podcast, we started to get nervous about the idea that we had to be funny in every episode. We realized that the times we didn't try to be funny were the times we were the funniest. When we were patient and just being ourselves, the hilarious moments came naturally and were funnier than if we tried to force a joke.

We don't know what the future holds, but we know that we cannot control it. Anxiety is trying to force things to happen in the future, and we quickly learned that we can't do that. The only thing we can control in this life is laughter. Let things unfold as they should and when they don't, just giggle.

IN CONCLUSION

WE THOUGHT THAT LAST SENTENCE was a pretty good ending, but we were told that we have to write a conclusion. Writing this is triggering because the last time we wrote a real conclusion was in high school, when Hannah had food in her braces and Paige was fighting rumors about spending her Limited Too modeling money on a secret mansion. But here we are, at the end of this book, and we guess it is only polite to say a formal farewell. But first, you should be proud of yourself for finishing a book, you fucking nerd. If you briefly skimmed the book and just wanted to see how it ends, you are equally welcome to enjoy this paragraph too.

In conclusion, please take everything we just said with a grain of spicy margarita salt. We know that we had very strong opinions on hand jobs, Scottsdale, and crying on Insta stories, but by the time this book is published, our lives and perspectives could be very different. For example, Hannah was destroying a guy wearing fur Crocs in the front row at a show and eight months later, fur Crocs became her entire personality. Somehow the day just got away from us and this book became a lot of advice and now we are nervous that you're all going to quit your jobs and your birth control and start a cult that meets at the Zara makeup section on Mondays.

Regardless of what you do, just make sure that you always commit to being delusional, decentering men, and never forgetting that your life is truly just one big silly bit. We love you so much. This was way too much admin. Thanks for giggling with us and for supporting women in the arts.

XOXO

Hannah & Paige

Your ex may have finished early, but we're not done yet . . .

A LIST OF OUR BITS

OOP WE'RE NOT DONE! Here are some of our favorite bits that we are fully committed to, with their origin story, definition, and common usage. We hope they help you calm your social anxiety and be the funniest person in the room!

WARNING, GIRLIES: If used out of context, like in a random elevator or meeting your boyfriend's parents for the first time, they may not work. Although, with the right parents, a well-timed "I'm a big fan of your work" might just get a laugh. But in our world of giggling, they are *chef's kiss* and can be used as code words to spot another Giggler in public and determine if they can be trusted.

ALLEGEDLY

ORIGIN: Whenever a reporter says something accusatory, they legally need to say "allegedly" so no one sees them in court (yes, we use a lot of legal jargon in our everyday life à la Elle Woods). We first started saying it during our Giggly Squad Instagram Lives when we were talking a lot about pop culture and did not want to get in trouble because it was during Covid and we were actually scared of everything.

DEFINITION: This is one of our all-time favorite bits. It allows us to tell you the most out-of-pocket, craziest, most exaggerated gossip and if three seconds after wrapping it up we say "allegedly," just know that it was a theatrical performance for our entertainment. You're welcome. You can also spill tea that you're not supposed to spill if you say "allegedly," because it suggests you can neither confirm nor deny *wink wink.*

USED IN A SENTENCE (HANNAH): Charlie Puth said I was the love of his life. Allegedly.

APPARENTLY

ORIGIN: Ingrained in our brains forever is an adorable eight-year-old, redheaded boy who went viral for an interview he did on local news where he said the word *apparently* way too many times. He sounded like all of us when we were writing an essay in high school and had to hit a certain word count.

DEFINITION: The word means what it means, but when you say the word *apparently*, you have to do justice to this young redheaded boy and say it in his voice. Using his accent adds texture to your already long-winded story and will make this bit hilarious to anyone who has seen this viral video.

USED IN A SENTENCE (PAIGE): Apparently, Simone Biles's husband thinks he's more of a catch than Simone Biles, and apparently she loves him but they can't talk about who is better at sports or they get in a fight, and apparently she thinks one day he will be more successful than her. We still don't know his name.

CAPITALISM WINS AGAIN.

ORIGIN: We like to use this bit any time someone is talking about something we don't understand, which happens shockingly often. Money and taxes are confusing. Politics can be confusing, but one thing we know is that capitalism wins again. Is your dad asking you about your taxes? Capitalism wins again. Boss won't give you a raise? Capitalism wins again. We can also use this bit to justify any and all purchases. Buying Gen Z's TikTok recommendations isn't our fault—capitalism wins again!

DEFINITION: We live in an economic and political system in which our country's trade and industry are controlled by private owners for profit, and it's not our fault that we spent all our money.

USED IN A SENTENCE: I just bought snail mucin on TikTok Shop because one influencer who is naturally pretty said it made her skin feel soft. Capitalism wins again.

DECENTERING MEN FROM OUR LIVES

ORIGIN: Struggling to find love in their mid-twenties, Hannah and Paige realized that the moment they truly started focusing on themselves and what brings them joy, they gained confidence and they began to attract better guys. They don't chase, they attract!!! The second a guy starts affecting your mental health and your peace, he's out. Their mantra is to always decenter men from their lives because they will never lose who they are. Hannah is actually married, but it's very off-brand for her and she tries to keep it a secret.

DEFINITION: Do not let men distract you from being your true self or from focusing on your career! Don't let them bring you down while you're on your way up!

USED IN A SENTENCE:
PAIGE: Why isn't your husband in your wedding photos?
HANNAH: I'm decentering men from my life.

GET MY AFFAIRS IN ORDER

ORIGIN: Many smart people believe that the phrase originated during the plague, when people were advised to get their affairs in order in case they became infected and died.

DEFINITION: The phrase "get your affairs in order" refers to organizing one's personal and financial matters, such as creating a will, identifying an executor or trustee, and arranging for end-of-life care, including management of health care and personal financial and business matters, if necessary.

USED IN A SENTENCE
PAIGE: I overdosed on my acne medication and I told my mom to get my affairs in order.
HANNAH: As I was choking to death on Cheez-Its, I was thinking that I need to get my affairs in order.

GIRD YOUR LOINS.

ORIGIN: Since Giggly Squad is a Stanley Tucci stan account, we remember this expression fondly as one of his most iconic and underrated lines from *The Devil Wears Prada*. So of course we use it often on the pod.

DEFINITION: According to the Bible, it means you need to prepare for battle by pulling up your robe and tying it around your waist so you can move with ease, fight, run, and ride your horse comfortably. We enjoy saying this right before we lay some superhot gossip in the group chat.

USED IN A SENTENCE (HANNAH): I just ate a chicken parmigiana and forgot to take my Lactaid pill. Gird your loins.

I APOLOGIZE TO THE ACADEMY.

ORIGIN: Will Smith famously slapped Chris Rock across the face during the 2022 Academy Awards. He later apologized to the Academy for his actions, but the Academy banned him from any awards shows for ten years.

DEFINITION: You are very sorry for your actions.

USED IN A SENTENCE
PAIGE: Why did you tell everyone that you were doing natural-nail summer and then went full French acrylic?
HANNAH: I apologize to the Academy.

I (WE, THEY) CAN'T BE MANAGED.

ORIGIN: One thing that really connects the Gigglers is the inability to be managed in any situation. Although originated by Kanye West, it is a foundational aspect of being a Giggler. In fact, it was the first major Giggly Squad bit that we made into merch! A perfect moment to use this bit? Anytime someone is trying to reprimand you or tell you what to do. This can be as simple as your boss asking you why you're forty-five minutes late while you are holding an iced coffee. Your response is quick and to the point, you simply state, "I can't be managed." It's clear at this moment by the look on their face that your "boss" does not support women in the arts or STEM, to be honest.

DEFINITION: No matter the rules, laws, parenting, grammar, or social norms, we go astray. This behavior is not usually malicious;

we just can't get our act together, most of the time. People who can't be managed live their lives to the beat of their own drummer, as they say.

USED IN A SENTENCE:
HANNAH: Why didn't you wear pants to BravoCon?
PAIGE: I can't be managed.

I DON'T DO ADMIN.

ORIGIN: We hate supporting men in the arts, but this phrase actually originated from Hannah's tall ex-boyfriend, British Dave. She asked him if he was upset that England lost the war to America, and he shrugged and said, "America was too much admin. We were running so many countries at the time, we really didn't care."

This really stuck with Hannah because she realized that, similar to when the British Empire was at its height of colonial power and started to lose track of all the stuff they were in charge of, she also cannot do admin. At all. Ever. From forgetting to call a plumber to letting her license expire, things just don't get done. Our favorite recollection of her not doing admin is when Hannah accidentally canceled her husband's six-hour international flight to Ireland because she simply could not stop clicking the wrong prompts. Or when she left the post office in tears when she tried to mail a Christmas present to her brother. That package is still sitting in her apartment.

DEFINITION: The inability to complete a simple, administrative task. Everything and anything can be admin if it requires more than one step, memory, or talking to strangers. Cleaning, packing, making plans, opening mail or packages, laundry, paperwork, paying your taxes. Life is so hard.

USED IN A SENTENCE:
PAIGE: Did you call 911 when Des thought he was having a heart attack?
HANNAH: I don't do admin.

IF I HAD A NICKEL.

ORIGIN: This bit comes from the term "if I had a nickel for every time [fill in the blank] I'd be rich" coined (no pun intended) by Mark Twain and then used in countless movies, songs, and conversations. To prove she's not like other girls, Hannah started to say, "If I had a nickel."

DEFINITION: Use this bit to talk about things that happen extremely often or to talk ironically about things that rarely happen. We like to use it for the exact opposite: it really throws people off and has them essentially questioning everything about you.

USED IN A SENTENCE
HANNAH: I just sharted in a bodega.
PAIGE: If I had a nickel.

I WAS READING THE *NEW YORK TIMES*. . . .

ORIGIN: Hannah and Paige get all their information from TikTok. Therefore, whenever they try to discuss anything, their only source of any knowledge is from TikTok, but they call it the *New York Times*, because they are embarrassed, uncultured swine.

DEFINITION: Doomscrolling TikTok for several hours and having never read the *New York Times*.

IN A SENTENCE (PAIGE): I was reading the *New York Times* and it said that the aesthetic of the season is electric grandpa.

I WISH THEM WELL.

ORIGIN: Since this is a ski podcast, we have to reference Gwyneth Paltrow's iconic ski trial. A man tried to sue her for a ski accident and she countersued for $1 because she has too much money. When she won the trial, she walked by him and whispered, "I wish you well." This was so nice and so mean at the same time. This is the perfect answer when you can't say how you really feel about someone and you don't want to get in trouble for talking shit.

DEFINITION: You do not wish them well.

USED IN A SENTENCE
HANNAH: I heard that your ex-boyfriend just got engaged.
PAIGE: I wish them well.

MY LOVE

ORIGIN: Hannah posted a clip from her *Berning In Hell* podcast. The video went viral, and the next day Hailey Bieber DMed Hannah. Hannah froze in fear. Not knowing how to respond or how to address this icon, Hannah panicked and called her "my love."

DEFINITION: When you don't know what to call another girlie but you are obsessed with her and want to make sure she loves you back.

USED IN A SENTENCE (HANNAH IN EVERY GIRLS' BATHROOM): Hi, my loves! Who needs a tampon?

NICHE

ORIGIN: Hannah likes to use this term when she makes a joke that no one understands. Paige likes to use it when she's trying to explain something on the pod and it is not making any sense.

DEFINITION: When someone just wouldn't understand something and you truly cannot take the time to explain it. For example, if any man asks you to explain a single ounce of pop culture you can respond, "Oooh it's so niche, I'm not sure you'd understand." This response completely throws them off because it really is not the definition of niche.

USED IN A SENTENCE
HANNAH AT A PARTY: Did you see the cult documentary where the leader said she could speak to Robin Williams and when someone didn't listen to her she would tell them that Robin Williams is angry?

CRICKETS

HANNAH: Okay, that was niche.

NO NOTES

ORIGIN: When you work in a creative field, you will submit a project to your boss (whether it's a video, copywriting, or any kind of content). If they don't like it, they will give notes for feedback and editing, but if they approve it exactly as is, they say, "No notes."

DEFINITION: You are obsessed and it is perfection and no changes should ever be made. It is the perfect quick Instagram comment to leave on a photo of your bestie. We also joke that sometimes people say "No notes" when they haven't listened to a single thing someone has vented about in the past thirty minutes and they do not want to get caught. This can be dangerous though because you could have just signed off on some of the craziest text messages being sent, but reading is not in our job description.

USED IN A SENTENCE
HANNAH: What do you think of my Zara set?
PAIGE: No notes.

SEE YOU IN COURT (SMALL CLAIMS VERSUS SUPREME)

ORIGIN: Apparently, legally it has no meaning, but people will use the phrase "I will see you in court" to threaten someone with the fear of litigation. It means that they are going to file a suit against you and you have to face the consequences in a court of law. Judge Judy, our Lord and savior, has probably said it before.

DEFINITION: Seeing someone in court is the ultimate "fuck around and find out." When you think something is wrong, messed up, or strongly disagree, you can respond with "See you in court." If the situation is very specific and not that big of a deal, you can say "small-claims court," but if it is horrific, then you say "supreme court." The "level of court" depends purely on your passion for the subject. For example, if you are starving and your Uber Eats delivers to the wrong apartment, that's a sound-enough argument in our opinion to be brought to supreme justice.

PAIGE: She did a whole get-ready-with-me video and didn't mention one brand she used.
HANNAH: See you in small-claims court.
HANNAH: He ordered spaghetti with a cup of milk.
PAIGE: See you in the supreme court.

SHE DIDN'T EVEN LEAVE A LASAGNA.

ORIGIN: Hannah's cousin Kara was explaining how her friend did something really messed up and didn't even leave a lasagna at her doorstep. This is a form of apology that is customary for Italians. Now Hannah and Paige use the phrase every time they feel they've been wronged.

DEFINITION: When someone wrongs you and doesn't sufficiently apologize by giving you a savory Italian layered pasta cake that will make you shit yourself in the best way.

USED IN A SENTENCE
PAIGE: Can you believe that Ciara wore a bathing suit to your wedding?
HANNAH: Yeah, and she didn't even leave a lasagna.

THAT NEVER CAME ACROSS MY DESK.

ORIGIN: We don't know anything about corporate America, but we feel like this is something you would say in a meeting when your manager is asking about a task or business thingy and you have no idea what they are talking about but probably should.

DEFINITION: Shoot, I have no idea what you're talking about or I simply just forgot to listen. What's funnier is if there are no desks involved in the making of this bit. You can also use it to avoid answering a difficult or controversial question.

USE IN A SENTENCE
HANNAH: Do you know how to open the door of a Tesla?
PAIGE: That never came across my desk.

WOMEN IN THE ARTS

ORIGIN: I guess we heard someone say "Women in the arts" to describe something professional like acting at Juilliard.

DEFINITION: In this context, "Women in the arts" means literally anything women do. If someone says something about a woman's actions that is negative, you can ask them why they don't support women in the arts.

USED IN A SENTENCE
HANNAH: Stephanie was gossiping all night about her ex-situationship.
PAIGE: Do you not support women in the arts?

Thanks for giggling with us <3

ACKNOWLEDGMENTS

Special thanks to Lenore Berner for holding
our hand through this process
and to Grace for existing
and to any giggler that made it this far in the book.